THE NEXT STEP:

York Preparatory Academy English 4 Reflections

Tiffany DiMatteo, editor

Foreword by Dr. T.K. Kennedy

English 4 students of York Preparatory Academy reflect on their lives and futures in individual essays.

TABLE OF CONTENTS

Foreword by Dr. T.K. Kennedy — 6
Introduction — 8

THE PAST

Dancing My Way through Life by Morgan Abercrombie — 10
Dirty Hands, Clean Money by Taylor Adkins — 11
The Big Push by Sean Allen — 14
They Lie by Erin Anderson — 16
Clothes Make the Woman by Jaylen Barkley — 18
"Mom, May I Go to the Bathroom?" by Peyton Brumfield — 20
Into the River by Randy Cyphers — 23
Just Me and You by Daelin Duran — 25
Cutting into Life by Lauren Forsythe — 28
Dear Freshman Me by Emma Gargiulo — 30
Racing to the Finish Line by Hailey Hawkins — 32
Scout's Honor by Landon Hoffman — 34
The Game of Life by Kelsey Hudson — 36
It's Not Me, It's You by Rosie James — 38
The Exceptional Student by Jared A. Key — 40
Building My Future by John LeBrun — 42
It's Written All Over You by Nia Lindsay — 45
My Garden by Madi Mott — 47
Impossible=I'm Possible by Elizabeth Nunn — 49
Stepping into the Unknown by Timothy Sanders — 51
Not All Who Wander Are Lost by Emilee Stohl — 52
Beyond Labels by Jake Thomson — 55
Origin Story by Maiah Whitehead — 56

THE PLAN

College and Career by Tyler Billings — 60
Fifteen Lessons by Peyton Chappell — 61

Overtime by Tracus Chisholm	64
The Second Quarter of My Life by Khali Clegg	66
My Future by Brittany Crisp	68
I Can't Wait by Jordan Faulkenberry	69
Creating a Better Future by Katelyn Forsythe	72
My New Chapter by Victoria Gaston	73
Jumping into the Unknown by Jonathan Grant	75
Taking the Shot by Monta Houston	76
"Make Many Plans" by Maddy Knox	79
My Pinterest Bucket List by Aubrie Midkiff	80
Resilience, Patience, Guidance by Mallory Pannell	83
Making Life Beautiful by Brandi Patterson	85
Private Ethan by Ethan Richardson	86
The Lessons We Learn by Devin Scott	88
"It Won't Be Like This for Long" by Emma Smith	91
My Perfectly Glazed Doughnut by Elena Walrod	94
The Pug Life by Rachel Youngblood	96

THE DREAM

Wet Socks by Austin Ball	99
The African Dream by Chloe Craig	101
My Fallout Life by Matthew Culver	103
To My Future Child(ren) by Morgan Foster	105
The Fantasy by Danielle Hancock	107
I Want to be a Writer…by Kevin Hicks	109
Dreaming of a New Future by Meghan Joseph	111
I Will by Max Kennington	112
Mid-life Contemplation by Jake Lowman	114
The Sound of My Music by Sam McCloud	117
The Future Is Mine by Maia Morrison	119
Hello, Little Me by Elain Moses	121
Call Me Sam by Hannah Smith	123
The Art of Life by Allie Tkach	126

Lancer by Eric Wells 128

THE UNKNOWN

I'm Not A... by Nathan Ballew 131
Twenty by William Binkley 132
Onward & Upward by Cooper Brown 134
This Cookie Doesn't Crumble by Noah Cooke 136
But What Now? by Jacob Emmons 138
Going for Goal by Michael Gleaves 140
The Movie of My Life by Chelsea Ingalls 142
Life Is a Journey by Emily Jackson 145
The Happy Step by Eron Johnson 147
The Path by Kameron Midkiff 149
21st Century Scop by Troy Ray 150
Plastic Sparkly Sandals by Annie Robinson 152
I Breathe, I Think, I Dream by Ella Rosenberg 155
Santa, the Tooth Fairy, and My Future by Rosie Torres 157
What to Do? by Bailey Youngs 159

POSTSCRIPT

The End Is Just the Beginning 162

Foreword by Dr. T.K. Kennedy

Lately, it seems that the news and other media outlets have focused on informing the public about the negative things involving our teenagers. However, many who serve in the education field with teenagers know that young people across this country are doing amazing things in their communities and abroad. There is an old saying in our society: "The children are our future." If we truly believe that statement, we must provide children with more opportunities to develop their own points of view and express themselves. Hopefully, this manuscript provided our students with the means to be heard.

Nothing is more pleasing than to serve as principal to these talented teenage authors while they navigate through their individual thoughts and reflections in this book. Webster defines 'reflection' as *1. An image that is seen in a mirror or on a skinny surface. 2. Something that shows the effect, existence, or character of something else. 3. Something that causes people to disapprove of a person or thing.* In these essays, each author identifies with at least one of the three definitions within the text. Most importantly, the reader will discover the students' skill level to think critically and evaluate incidents that are important to each of them. These thought-provoking essays are expressed in a manner that forces the reader to reflect and connect on a personal level, regardless of age.

Under the guidance of their English teacher Tiffany DiMatteo, students were led on a journey to reflect individually and to collaborate on a text for the world to peruse. She has empowered them to have a voice on various viewpoints surrounding their personal beliefs, concerns, and opinions about the past, present, and the future.

Some of these authors will use this book-publishing experience and feeling of accomplishment to lead them down a clear career path or educational pursuit. Others will continue to write or produce more published works in the future. No matter what may happen in their very bright futures, we are incredibly proud of these students and the work produced in this volume.

Introduction

As I sit back and take a deep breath to admire the work of these students, the realization hits that there has been so much pressure to get their writing on the page that I forgot about my share: the privilege of introducing their work to the world.

The chapters in this book were individually written by English 4 students at York Preparatory Academy, a K-12 charter school in Rock Hill, South Carolina. YPA was born in 2010 and had its first graduating class of seniors in 2015; the authors of this book will graduate in 2016 and 2017. The idea of a collaborative book was presented to them, we brainstormed topics and themes, narrowed down and voted on the top three, and we arrived on a theme that would appeal to almost everyone. There were students who wanted to write about the future and those who wanted to write about the past as an influence on the future. In addition, there were students who wanted to write more creatively, and, of course, those who didn't know what to write. However, through the process, the students realized that they all had interesting and significant things to say about their lives, and this text exists as a testament to their experiences and their ambitions.

These students had the indescribable pleasure of having me as their teacher (and learning how verbal irony is implemented in the classroom to uproarious comic effect). After thirteen years as a teacher, my students have been guided through literary analysis, creative writing, argumentative research, and Socratic seminar, but never through work that would certainly be published. I consider myself the ultimate appreciator of the literary arts because I have no interest in writing the next Great American Novel or Must-Read Memoir. When the school broached the topic of class-level projects, there was some panic, fear, and anxiety—from me, not the students. There was the burden of not only fitting it into the curriculum, but how? When? Do I press it on them at the beginning to get it over with? Or wait a little while until I know them and have a better sense of their preferences and abilities? Concern over high-stakes testing seems inconsequential when I have classrooms of teenagers with a publication date on the line.

But here it is: the book is ready for publication and to be shared with the world. Thank you to the parents and relatives who have raised these amazing kids, and for contributing to these stories, directly or indirectly. Thank you to the faculty and staff at YPA who have helped to make these young men and women who they are today. And to my students, my authors: I am so proud of the work you have done and the pieces of yourselves you are showing the world through your words. It has been such a privilege to guide you through this process. I can't wait for the ten year reunion to look back on this volume with you all—and we will dance the Sneaky Fish.

Tiffany DiMatteo

THE PAST

Dancing My Way through Life by Morgan Abercrombie
As I sit in the dance studio waiting for my next class to start, I start to wonder about what my life be like next year. I won't be at the dance studio everyday doing what I love, or even making inside jokes with my dance family. I won't be dancing my heart out on the stage, letting all of my feelings go. My life is going to be so different. Will I be able to survive without dance? What will I do with all of my free time? All of these thoughts run through my head every day of my senior year of high school.

I've been dancing for thirteen years and doing competition dance for ten years. Dance is the only sport that I have been able to stick with throughout my years in school. Last year, some of my best friends at dance graduated and it really hit me that I would be in their shoes the next year. I saw them cry, I cried with them, but I didn't understand that scared, nervous, and sad feeling that I am feeling this year. This year, I dance as if each day is my last time dancing and I know that in a couple of months, it will be totally different. Dance will be over! What will I do?

A dance studio is a very important part of the dance life. You have to make sure it's the right one for you and that you feel like the people there are your family. I started dance when I was three years old at Fascinating Rhythm in York, South Carolina. I loved dance, but when it came time for the day of the recital, I can remember not wanting to dance at all. I cried my eyes out, but my parents told me that I would be letting the other dancers down if I didn't dance, and I was going to finish what I had started. I ended up dancing at the recital and I am so glad that I did, because now dance is all I do and think about. The next year I ended up taking a few years off from dance to pursue cheerleading for the YMCA. I cheered for about two years and started dance again when I was in the second grade for Sullivan Dance Studio in Rock Hill. Sullivan then asked me to try out for their competition team. I was super scared, but my parents told me that I should at least try it, and that if I didn't like it I could just keep doing recreational classes. I made the team and loved it. My seventh grade year, Sullivan stopped doing a competition team, and decided to only have recreational classes. I knew that I still wanted to do competition, so I moved studios to Dance by Sherri in Rock Hill. I only danced there for a year because there was a lot of drama that interfered with my dancing. My eighth grade year, I moved to Step South Dance in Rock Hill.

After several studios, I figured out that Step South was the place for me to live out my love for dance. I still dance on the competitive team at Step South. We compete at four competitions a year, and do either nationals or a big trip during the summer. I have done almost all types of dance, but I currently take jazz, contemporary, hip hop, musical theater, and ballet. I am usually at the studio practicing four hours a day, Monday through Thursday. Lindsey Farris, my dance teacher and Step South's owner, has made me the person and dancer that I am today. Mrs. Lindsey has shown me her love of dance and makes me love dance even more every day. Without Mrs. Lindsey, I don't think I would still be dancing in high school, and now I never want dance to end. She has taught me to be the person that I am and not to hold back from anything because one day you will regret the chances that you didn't take, and she is right. I wish in my past years that I wouldn't have held back from things, such as not dancing to my full potential in class, and only dancing full out on stage. She teaches me how to be the person that I really am. Mrs. Lindsey is a great person and definitely someone that I look up to. She has made a huge impact on my life, and I'm very thankful for her. Step South is one big family, and I am so glad that I have been able to be a part of it for the last five years.

Throughout my years in school, people would always ask me, "What do you want to be when you grow up?" My response would always be a dance teacher. I wanted to own my own dance studio and teach people dance, and make them love it as much as I do. When I was in about tenth grade, I changed my mind. I didn't want to be a dance teacher anymore because I saw how much stress it was for Mrs. Lindsey. She would spend hours at the dance studio, arranging music, making and getting props, picking out the perfect costumes for each dance, and, worst of all, dealing with all of the parents. I didn't really want to give up dancing all together, but I didn't want to major in it. I plan on going to York Technical College after graduation, I plan on majoring in dental hygiene and teaching dance on the side at Step South.

All of my friends who have graduated and don't dance anymore tell me how much I will miss dance when it is all over. I am now getting those feelings and don't ever want dance to end. I know that I will probably be at the studio every day because my sister will still be dancing, but it won't be the same. My sister is twelve, and I don't think she loves dance as much as I do, but she still has lots of years to go. I pray that she will love it more as she gets older and when her days of dance come to an end, and she will never want it to end either.
I am so thankful that I have had the opportunity to dance. I am so thankful for the amazing group of dancers that I have been blessed to dance with, and my amazing dance teacher. I will always love dance and cherish all of the great memories. I hate that it has to come to an end, but I will always remember my years of dance.

*****

Dirty Hands, Clean Money by Taylor Adkins
It's 5:00 a.m., my mom's alarm clock goes off, and she yells, "Taylor, it's time to get up! Go and get your brothers and sisters up and get to the barn." I slowly roll out of bed and get my work clothes and boots on, and then proceed down

the hallway and turn the lights on in each of my siblings' rooms. In the first room, there is Tucker, who is fifteen, and Roy, who is eight. In the second room, there is Ruth, thirteen, and Mary, eleven. I also have an older sister named Sam who is twenty-two, but she doesn't live with us anymore. And I have a three year old brother named Zeb, but we all call him Zebby. Now, I know what you're thinking: this is child labor. Well, it's not. It's how my family makes a living, and it's been this way since 1909. Farming, working hard, earning what we have, making the best of what we have, and praising God through the good and the bad is what I know and what I have been taught throughout my life by my parents.

By now, it is 5:30 and I have already eaten my bowl of oatmeal and I am headed to the barn. Once I get there, I start setting up the milk equipment, which is what we use to milk the cows and bottle the milk. Not only do we milk twenty-six cows, but we also milk twenty-three goats. We have many other types of animals, also. All together we have over sixty dairy cows, fifty or so goats, a heap of chickens, a few turkeys, pigs, five dogs, one cat, and one paint horse named Classic. Each and every one of the cows and goats have names. I am often asked how I remember which one is which; the truth is that I raised them from babies and they all have their own personalities. They aren't unintelligent as some people may portray them to be. I used to have a cow named Daisy and she loved people. She would treat my brothers and sisters like she was their mother, and she would follow you around everywhere and moo at you as well. Right now, I have a goat named Minnie and she was born with deformities: she is blind in one eye, her jaw is out of place and she is deaf in one ear. We didn't think she would make it as long as she has, but she is a little over a year old now, and she thinks she is a dog because she will follow you everywhere and she'll come when you call her.

Honestly, some days I wish I could just be a normal kid, but I wouldn't be who I am today without the values instilled in me at such a young age. When I was younger, I thought everyone lived on a farm or that they at least had a few animals. In elementary school, I realized that wasn't true and I was afraid that I would get picked on because I wasn't like everyone else. I always hear people complaining about what time they wake up in the morning or how they didn't get to go and hang out with their friends because they had to watch their siblings. Sometimes I just want to say "You're lucky!" I wish all I had to do was take out the trash or walk the dog, but then I realize that I have gotten so many great opportunities from being a dairy farmer. I used to be on a Guernsey quiz bowl team, which is a group of teenagers who learn facts about Guernsey cows and the significance of the dairy industry. We would study and memorize all kinds of facts that were constantly changing, and when the time came, we would be put up against another team and the judges would ask questions. Whoever hit the buzzer first could answer and if you were correct, your team got the points. If not, the other team got a chance to answer and so on. our quiz bowl team was able to go to a different state every summer and we would compete against many other teams from all over the country. I have been to Oregon, Oklahoma, Texas, Indiana, and Pennsylvania, to name a few. There are lots of upsides to being a farmer. You learn responsibilities, such as how to care for animals, grow crops, and make good decisions, because it could mean the difference between life and death. You also get to see the beautiful creations that God has made every day.

Many people tell me that they wish they had my life. However, they don't realize the sacrifices you have to make and the long hours it takes to run a farm. They don't know the heartbreak that comes when you stay up all night with a sick animal that doesn't survive. For example, I had a heifer calf named Rebel that was born on a cold, rainy day. We like to leave the calves with their mother until they are ready to be weaned. Not long after, I realized that she wasn't getting up and drinking as quickly as the other calves were, so I went out into the pasture and picked her up and carried her into the barn so I could give her some colostrum and get her warm. By doing this, I hoped she would be ready to go back out to her mother the next morning. I soon realized that there was something more serious that was wrong with her. She had a strained muscle in her neck that wouldn't allow her to lay her head down normally, so we called the vet and asked him to come out and take a look at her. He gave her some medicine and for a few months following, everything seemed okay. She would drink a whole bottle of milk, and she liked to get out to play in the sun. Then, one day, everything changed. She started holding her head weirdly again, so we gave her more medicine; however, it didn't work this time the way that it had before. Not too long after that, she had a seizure and passed away. She was around six months old, and by that time, we had realized the reason she had been acting funny—her brain didn't receive enough oxygen when she was born. It was very hard to see this happen after I had spent so much time and effort trying to get her better, but I guess that death is a part of life, too.

As I get older, I realize that living on a farm has helped shape me into the girl I am today. I am able to do many things that other kids my age would never even think of doing. For example, when I turned fifteen I wanted to have my own truck like my big sister, but unlike most parents nowadays, my mom and dad wouldn't just buy a truck and give it to me—they said I had to work for it. So, I started saving my money from working odd jobs and I bought my first truck. It needed a lot of work, so I had to save up even more money to fix it. I then found another truck that I really liked, so my parents bought it and then sold it to me. The truck seemed fine at first, aside from a knock you could hear in the motor. My dad checked it out and come to find out it had been run hot. So, I saved up the money and my dad and I rebuilt the motor and got it back on the road. Working all the time on the farm, it would be hard to get time to work on my truck, so it took about a year to get it back going. Sometimes we would be in the shop until almost midnight, and somedays, we didn't get to work on it at all. After it was all said and done, there were many hours of labor, greasy clothes, bloody knuckles from hitting them while taking bolts out, over two thousand dollars' worth of parts, lots of knowledge being learned, friends coming over to help out, and the chance to learn the trade of my dad and the patience it takes to take something apart and put it back together. My truck still isn't completely finished. I am still working to buy new interior things, as well as a suspension lift kit, and new tires. One thing I can say is, when you work really hard for something, you care a lot more about it.

My life isn't easy, and I might complain, but I love it. I know that one day when I have to get a job, I will be able to do that job to the best of my ability, because that is what being a farmer's daughter has taught me. I was asked to write this essay about the steps that I will take next in my life. Well, my next step is to be a hardworking, knowledgeable, honest, trustworthy, and respectful young woman. Part of that next step will be for me to be a light in an otherwise darkening world full of sin and hate. As it says in Matthew 5:14-16: *"You are the light of the world. A city on a hill cannot be hidden. Nor do people light a lamp and put it under a basket, but on a stand, and it gives light to all in the house. In the same way, let your light shine before others, so that they may see your good works and give glory to your Father who is in heaven."* I hope that if you have read this essay all the way to the end, that you have learned something about farmers. If you see a farmer, go and shake her hand and say thank you for all she does, and you might just make her day.

*****

The Big Push by Sean Allen

"In my future, I see myself going to college." That's most likely the answer every student gives about his/her future. If you take a survey and ask everyone what they want to do after high school, most students will say college. About 80% of students will say they will plan to go to college and 20% of those students will go to the military or take over the family business. But do those 80% of students actually make it to college? Do they know that it takes hard work and dedication to get colleges to at least look at your profile? Or do they think it will be easy and that their parents will do all of the work for them?

I plan on going to college and I am determined to make it there. Lately I have been visiting colleges with my dad like Duke, which was a great experience but has a very competitive acceptance rate. The college I want to go to is University of South Carolina. I haven't yet toured the college, but I plan to in January.

In the future I want practice in the medical field. Since I was middle school I've wanted to be a dentist. I want to be a dentist because I shadowed a dentist and I was amazed at the work they do other than cleaning teeth; they pull out teeth and give shots, too. I realized I wanted to be a dentist because I felt that it was perfect for me and I can see myself doing that in the future. I know that being a dentist will take hard work and determination, but I know that I can do it. When I was shadowing, I realized that dentists have less to worry about than regular doctors, because they focus on the mouth and not any other body part. I obviously knew that, but I never realized it. I know that the University of South Carolina has a good medical school and I plan on attending it in the future.

In high school, I've noticed there are three kinds of students. The first type are the people who always get good grades. Sometimes they don't try at all and they still have a high average in that class. I have friends who talk all class and when it comes to a test, they ace it with ease. Sometimes I'm amazed at how well that works. I wouldn't say that I'm jealous of those people, but it would make life a lot easier. I have a few friends that just goof off the whole class and they still pass tests and quizzes, while I'm over here actually paying attention and still struggling on the topic. In high school you also have those students that don't care for school at all. They don't put in effort at all. They get bad grades and act like it was nothing. I would wonder what their parents are like, if they aren't concerned about daughters or sons.

Finally you have those students who try and study and still struggle, and I would consider myself one of those students. I wouldn't say I'm bad at school, it's just difficult knowing that school isn't my strong point. I could study for hours and hours and still not get what I'm even reading; the only way I can actually get the lesson is with the help of my dad, who is a big part of my life. Half of the time when I pass a quiz or test, it's because of the help of my dad. Sometimes I hate asking my dad for help because I want to be able to learn and study by myself, but I have no other choice. To me it's either study with someone who has more experience studying on his own or fail the next quiz or test. My dad has a pretty cool job--he flies undercover airplanes for the FBI. But flying for the FBI means that you have to learn how to fly an airplane, and in order to do that, he studied on his own for five years. That's what I want to be able to do. When I have my dad help me to study he has this strategy called "Alphabet Soup". This means looking for words that relate to the answer. It's a pretty cheap way of knowing the information, but it works most of the time.

It's especially hard to study when your only way of passing a test is out of town. Being in the FBI, my dad travels a lot and it's really hard to study over the phone. Sometimes if I have to, I even ask my mom for help, but it can be a struggle--she doesn't know how to pronounce some of the words because English isn't her first language. Originally my mom is from the Philippine Islands. My dad met her when he was stationed there while he was in the Navy. They got married there and my dad brought her to the United States.

It's very difficult to have her help me, so I just end up trying to study by myself.

When I take tests or quizzes I always feel pressured because of my dad. My dad is a good person, but he is also a strict person. Every time I fail or mess up in school, I feel like I disappoint him every time. When I take the test I always think about the consequences waiting for me at home. What if I disappoint him even more? My whole life I've been pressured to do good in school. My dad had a hard childhood. He grew up with fourteen brothers and sisters, so he had to share a bed with four other siblings. He had to work in Missouri in the corn fields with his other siblings day and night. I can see why my dad pushes my so hard--because he wants me to have a better life than he did, and I don't blame him. If I had children I would want them to be better than me. In life, my main goal is to make my dad proud of me.

In the end, I am most grateful for what I have. I know that lots of kids would love to have a mom and dad that pushes them in school and in life. Some people don't realize how lucky they are to have parents that care and push them to do well. At the end of college I want to say that I wanted to go to college and I succeeded--not only that my parents pushed me, but because I pushed myself.

*****

They Lie by Erin Anderson

"Senior year will be the best year of your life," they said. Oh, and I believed it, too.

I had fantasized about my senior year since I was in kindergarten--it was supposed to be this great year full of fun, and cherishing everything before it would come to a sad but exciting end. However, a couple of weeks in and my dreamy state came to an abrupt halt, and the realization that this year was not going to go the way I expected quickly flooded in.

College preparation began and the future was right there in a single application. Right then, I was forced with the task of deciding where it was I could see myself living for the next four years of my life. Where it was I would be attending school in less than a year, and whether or not I was even good enough to get into the schools I wanted to go to in the first place. But this stress of the future wasn't my main concern. Without even noticing, I became swept up in the complications of my own personal life. It seemed as though everything began to fall apart. My family, my friends, everything. I couldn't even sit down long enough to catch my breath before something else was falling off of my metaphorical shelf and crashing to the ground. I was constantly trying to hold on to the past and the present, but for nothing that would benefit me in the future. Because what on earth is the point of thinking about the future when I can't even come to terms with what's happened in the past and what is going on in the present?

As I began my senior year I felt on top of the world. My friend group felt strong and ready to take on our last year at school together. However, it quickly ended. My friends have a pretty significant impact on me, especially ones I have been close to for a long time. Seeing someone turn against you so quickly, disregarding years of memories, vacations, and traditions, was a strong slap in the face. I found myself feeling helpless. No matter how hard I tried, nothing was fitting together anymore; my relationships were falling apart and there wasn't anything I could do to fix it. I was desperately looking for someone to just talk to, someone who felt as lonely as I did, or sad as I did. Someone who would reassure me that the lies, and the retaliation coming from these toxic friendships were in fact that, lies.

This is where I really learned that growing up sucks. It has become this romanticized idea that we are all living this story of overcoming hardship and allowing it to mold us to be a different, stronger person who will go out and change the world for the better. However, this may not always be the case. Not everyone comes to the day where a sudden beautiful realization overcomes you to where they think to themselves that they're going to be okay and that the world is happy place. For many, and for me in particular, this wasn't the way it happened. I had multiple moments where I thought this way, and then was quickly disappointed when I fell right back into the sad state I was in before. Every day there is struggle--every day there is something there to remind us that life isn't always going to go the way we want it to, our senior year isn't always going to run as smoothly as we were told, and the people we love aren't always going to love us back.

Separating the past, the present, and the future was when I had to grow up. Just to be clear, this wasn't some grand moment for me, where I realized that growing up is all a beautiful part of life. It was hard. I was stuck in a Peter Pan state of mind, avoiding the future and clinging to anything that kept me happy. Whether it was toxic friendships or old feelings that used to make me feel good, I grasped onto them because I thought I needed them to take the next steps into my future. However, begrudgingly and painfully, I found a way to attempt to put my feelings in their place, deciding whether my circumstances should follow me into the next phase of life, or if they were to be left in the past. And this is much easier said than done. There is an unfortunate thing that most human beings tend to do: let our circumstances affect us. I spent months of my senior year letting myself be sad, and allowing every possible thing that went wrong to sneak into my mind and tear me down piece by piece.

I reached a point where I was doing what I thought was my best at finding peace in leaving things in the past, except all I ended up doing was constantly avoid any potentially painful reminders. The future became a bright light at the end of a long, dark tunnel that was my senior year. "You're almost there, Erin--just a few months more and you'll be away from all of it," I would continuously reassure myself. I started to use my circumstances to fuel me to make it to my last day of high school. I threw myself into college preparation, and counting down the days until the time for graduation would finally arrive. This may seem like a good thing, but I forgot to consider that my past wasn't fully dealt with. At any moment if I were reminded of something painful, all my hard-work and what I thought was progress could be pointless, and I'd be back where I started. It was similar to a scene in the movie *Cars*. Lightning McQueen was racing in a big race to win the Piston Cup. He decided he wasn't going to stop at any pit-stops to get new tires; he would just continue to fill up with gas and go, so he could get to the finish line first and win the race. I wasn't stopping to get new tires, I continued to fill up with gas and keep pushing on until eventually, like Lightning McQueen, my tires would go out, and I would be hopping my way to the finish line, hardly even able to get myself there. Dealing with the future may be ominous, but dealing with the past is painful. I did my best to avoid it until I had to determine that it was my time to grow up and deal with the things that made me feel sad, so that I could move on and be happy again.

When I finally sorted through my circumstances, looking back at the past became less of a haunting nightmare and rather a simple memory. Losing long-term friendships and having failed expectations was difficult and saddening; however, it may have been exactly what I needed--to let go of people that belonged in the past and leave them there. No matter how many disappointing things happened this year, they allowed me to find confidence in my future, and pushed me, although at first reluctantly, into my next steps of life. My year may not have been the ideal or perfect senior year, but it held many valuable lessons and allowed me to grow up and ready myself for the next chapter of my life. And I believe that that's the way growing up works--accepting that things won't always be perfect, but finding peace in it anyway and moving on in a better and more mature way than you would have before.

*****

Clothes Make the Woman by Jaylen Barkley

I was seven years old sitting on the couch watching TV at my aunt's house, waiting on my favorite cousin to come home from school. On this particular day, my aunt picked me up from my school because my mom was busy at work. This was not a problem for me because I always enjoyed being around my cousins, being that I was the only child. After what seemed like forever, Selena finally walked through the door wearing the same smile that I was and it seemed to get even bigger once she noticed me sitting on the couch. We automatically ran to each other, screaming like we hadn't been together in years, when in all actuality, it had only been a few days. As we were talking, I took in her outfit, which was a really cute pink GAP sweatsuit. I then looked down at my attire: a khaki skirt and a blue collared polo shirt with black uniform shoes. Realizing the major difference in our clothing, I couldn't help but feel down. I always wanted to dress cute like that, but attending private school required uniforms. Every now and then we had "dress up" days, where we could wear our own choice of clothing, but that still wasn't what I wanted. From that moment on, I was determined to convince my mom to let me go to public school.

School, for me, has always been a priority due to the fact that my mother is a tad bit of a pusher. Not the annoying kind of pusher where she makes me take all the classes she took, but more of the motivating type of pusher. The kind that encourages me to take challenging courses but does not force it. Starting in kindergarten, I attended a private school and continued private education up until third grade. Although I did not like the uniform aspect of private school, I can say that it gave me a lot of great characteristics and advantages. Being that I was so young, wearing uniforms didn't really bother me much in kindergarten. As I matured and began to adapt my own sense of fashion, my dislike for uniforms grew.

After a great amount of begging, pleading, and even some crying, I finally talked my mom into letting me attend a public school my third grade year. The school was close to our home and all of my friends from my neighborhood attended. Third grade was a good time because I finally got to wear whatever I wanted--but it also turned out to be somewhat of a disaster. I made many friends, and some of them I am still friends with now. However, the problem wasn't socially, it was in the classroom with my teacher. I was never disobedient; however, I was a bit talkative like every other third grader in our classroom. I always thought my teacher was a bit mean and for a while I excused it and just blamed it on her being strict. It wasn't until my mom and I found out that she had talked about me, along with a few other students, on Facebook. The coincidence, unfortunately, was that all the students she named were African American, and at that moment I realized she wasn't mean because she was strict, she was mean because she was prejudiced. After that, my mom instantly withdrew me from that school and found a new school for my fourth grade year. Although it was not the best school year, attending public school finally gave me a taste of freedom and made me even more of a social butterfly than I was before.

For fourth grade we returned back to private school and those hideous uniforms. Going into fourth grade was the definition of a bittersweet moment: I was excited to be at a new school and meeting new people, but I was not at all excited about being required to wear uniforms again. The school we chose for fourth grade was a lot smaller than the two private schools I'd previously attended. Traditionally, classes in private school are small, but at this school, third and fourth graders were all in one classroom. There were five students in total, two of them being third graders and the other three, including myself, were fourth graders. On the first day, when I walked into the classroom I thought I was super early because there were only four other people there; then my teacher explained that it was just the five of us. Having only four other students in my class was somewhat of an advantage because I experienced one-on-one teaching time that many other kids in public schools miss. Although fewer students in the room benefitted my education, it really did not strengthen my people skills.

Private school gets expensive very quickly, so in fifth grade my mom enrolled me at York Preparatory Academy. This was a great idea because it offered education equivalent to that of a private school, without the private school price. When I began at York Prep in 2010, it had just opened and was the only charter school in Rock Hill. The first day at YPA was very nerve wracking because I didn't really know what to expect, considering that anyone who lives in York County could apply and be accepted. After being at YPA for a few months, I kind of got into the groove of things and that made being there so much better. I became friends with so many people. Everyone at York Prep is unique, but it feels like a family, and that itself has made my time here so much more enjoyable.

I am now a sophomore in high school and also still a student at York Prep. I think York Prep is great; it has given me a sense of freedom because I can now wear my own clothes, no uniforms, and I am able to meet and build friendships with so many new people. My grades are great and attending YPA has put me at a great advantage, one so special that I could graduate a year early. Being that my mom is my biggest motivator, she's encouraged me to take classes beyond my grade level, because she believes I can handle it. The quality of education at my school is amazing; of course, it's not perfect, but what school is? York Prep doesn't just feel like a school; it feels more like a family. After I finish high school, I have plans to attend Spelman College, which is a private, female HBCU located in Atlanta, Georgia. I know you are probably thinking, "Another private school?" Well, yes. My dislike was not the private school itself, it was the uniforms. At Spelman uniforms are not required, so I think I'll be just fine. I even have a greater hope to become a trauma surgeon. There are many types of characteristics needed to be a trauma surgeon, like time management, hospitality, empathy, and the ability to meet and get along with different types of people. Taking all of the traits I've adapted from going to many different schools, I hope I can become one of the most caring and congenial trauma surgeons there is, and I will rock those blue scrubs better than anyone has ever done.

*****

"Mom, May I Go To the Bathroom?" by Peyton Brumfield
When I was younger, I always wanted to be older than I was. Looking back now, I wish I didn't think that way as a kid. When you're little, you never

realize how fast you are going to grow up and have to start being a responsible young adult. I really started wanting to be older than what I was around the age of ten. I showed that need with my bad behavior towards not only my parents but my teachers. This attitude towards grownups helped me learn many lessons just from this one experience at a young age. Let me be clear: I wasn't disrespectful to all of my teachers. I just felt like if a teacher didn't show me respect, I didn't need to show them respect. This way of thinking made it difficult for me and at least one of my teachers to see eye to eye each year. I went from the age of ten in fourth grade until the age of fifteen in ninth grade with the mindset that if a teacher didn't show me respect, I didn't have to respect them. I know now that this made school so much more difficult than it had to be. That experience of always having one teacher that I didn't respect made my life in school terrible for those years. I vividly remember not getting along with my fifth grade teacher at all. She was my homeroom teacher and I couldn't stand her (from what I remember, the feeling was mutual). Of course, now I couldn't tell you why I despised her. It's been so long ago and I'm sure it was over something dumb. The real problem I do remember was that my homeroom teacher and I not getting along affected my grades. That was when I began to realize it's better to just kill a teacher with kindness if you have to. That was definitely an experience that helped me realize that it makes school much easier when you get along with your teachers.

While I was in elementary school my mom worked for Kelly Services which is a program for substitute teachers. The problem with my mom being a substitute was that she frequently was hired to sub at my elementary school. I remember on several occasions my mom being the sub for my class. This started to become a problem because it's hard to treat the sub like a teacher when she's your mom and you live with her. Don't get me wrong, I definitely have respect for my mom, it's just strange to walk into class and have your MOM greet you at the door. What was even stranger was that she wanted me to call her "Mom" while she was the sub in my class. Imagine needing to use the bathroom during class and you have to raise your hand and say, "Mom, may I go to the bathroom?"

Throughout middle and high school, I have had many problems with administrators. In seventh grade, during recess, I decided to skip and go to the gym to play basketball. This was definitely a bad idea. It was the first time I had ever been written up and I was so scared. This experience put me in my place throughout middle school. In high school I got a little bolder in the second semester of my tenth grade year. I was taking Spanish II and my teacher had just passed out a worksheet. My friends and I had started saying, "I do what I want," and I got the bright idea to write "I do what I want" on the worksheet. My teacher saw it and got furious. She snatched the sheet off my desk and walked over to her desk. She then proceeded to take a picture of the sheet and sent it to the administrators. I was never called to the office but the administrators did write me up. This experience helped me understand how to be more professional in a classroom environment and not think everything is a joke.

Now that I am seventeen years old, I realized that life passes you by if you just sit back and worry too much about what everyone thinks. In my previous years as a high schooler I lived my life in the shadows, too worried about what others may think of me. As I have matured, I have learned not to care of what others think of me at all. High school is all about making experiences, finding yourself, and getting ready for your future.

For my senior year I want to make it a memorable one but also not forget what's most important: keeping my grades up. I have learned how important grades are through high school. I used to slack off in school and not worry about grades as much, but now I realize how important grades really are.

At the moment I'm not sure where I want to go to college. There are two reasons behind this; one being that I have no idea what I want to do for the rest of my life. The other being that every college campus has a different type of atmosphere and you should choose which one you feel you fit in with best. I have yet to go on an official college visit and hope to start visiting different colleges starting this coming spring. There are a two schools in particular I definitely want to visit. The first one being Western Carolina and the second being College of Charleston. If neither of these campuses seem like a fit for me, I'll just move on to different options.

Once I'm out of college I plan to get a job in my major. I know most people say life doesn't go how you plan it, but I have planned mine out. After I'm settled and have a good paying job, I hope to find a wife. I'm thinking of getting married at 26 and in two years have my first child. I definitely don't want to have a child before I'm settled because I want to be able to support my child. This may seem farfetched to try and plan out your life, but I've always felt like you need to know you can support a child before having one. Now don't take that the wrong way; these are just my morals and everyone has their own opinion. I'm not saying anyone's opinion is right or wrong. I just feel like to be the best dad I can be I should wait until I'm settled down.

The most important thing in my life right now is how I decide to live each day and to make sure all my decisions are responsible ones. I need to make sure I stay on track in school and always do my best work. Another thing I need to remind myself of are the lessons I have learned throughout my academic career so far. The first of those lessons being to always respect your teachers and professors even if they may not respect you. The second lesson is to always abide by the rules and never think you're above the rules that have been set in place. The most important of these lessons would definitely be to always remember to do what makes you happy and not worry about what everyone may think about you.

*****

Into the River by Randy Cyphers

After a very long journey up north to Ohiopyle, Pennsylvania, Kenya, Jeremy, PJ, Higgie, Greg, Becca, Sunshine, Jake, Rashid, Datko, and I arrived at the campsite well after dark. After being warned about the local wildlife, we got to our campsite, set up, and almost immediately fell asleep. The next morning I woke up knowing I was going to face my first class-five rapid--a large rapid with serious consequences--that day, and it was a scary feeling.

After the 45 minute car ride to the put-in of the upper Youghiogheny River, we slid our kayaks off the muddy bank and started down river. My best friend's dad noticed the face of a worried young paddler and started to give advice. "We have a couple miles of flatwater," he said, "so take this time to warm up. Imagine making these small little moves we are doing really big to wake the muscles up." I did just that--I started to over-exaggerate any little paddle stroke or hip movement, then I heard the best noise in the world: the rumbling of whitewater. I was told that I need to keep my kayak pointed perfectly downstream during the 15 foot slide. As we all started dropping off the slide, I see the hole (another name for a hydrolic in the river), and I keep my kayak pointed right at it and took the hardest paddle strokes I've ever taken in my life. As fast as I had started, I was through it and we had just dropped into the main gorge of this run. We had no idea any of the lines to run because most of the crew had only run it once before, so we ran the entire river, sometimes poaching lines from the commercial rafts that were chartering trips down the river.

After a couple or so miles we got to it: my first class-five rapid, Charley's Choice. I decided not to scout it because my nerves were totally shot. I was told it was a horseshoe shaped hole that was terminal, but to make matters worse there was a boulder smack dab in the middle of the hole, just small enough to crest out of the water. That boulder means you can't run through the middle so we pushed far right and subbed our boats out and to get spit out downstream. I was the third or so paddler in our group to run it, with one man out of the boat on a rock with a rope, just in case things go south. As I peel out of the eddie, I see my line as I approach the rapid. I get my first glimpse of the magnificent rapid that would ignite my passion for class five kayaking as I subbed out. Only my head and torso was above water and, just like a rocket, I accelerated away from the feature. I had done it! I felt like I was on top of the world--the thing I had spent so much time preparing for and fearing had paid off. The rest of the run was not over; there was a lot of fast-paced boulder gardens and lots of scouting, but we made it down the river safely. When we got to the take-out, we rejoined the rest of our friends and family, and went back to the campsite, ready for the next day to run an 18 foot waterfall. I didn't know it would change the way I viewed myself, the river, and kayaking overall.

There I was, landing the flattest boof of my life off of this magnificent cascade celebrating at the bottom of a job well done...and then I woke up. As I crawled out of the tent seeing most of group already awake, we went into town, ate some food, then went to the festival, ready for another amazing run. This waterfall is like no other: an 18 feet sloping boof into a very large flat pool below. This particular drop is usually only run once a year at the festival; unless you have three or more people, it's illegal to kayak there. Before I even saw this waterfall, I felt the earth rumbling like an earthquake from the amount of water cascading over it. Once I saw it, I got nervous, not out of fear, but anticipation. I have learned through my four years of kayaking that a little fear is good--it's healthy for every man and woman to have respect for the river.

There were a couple of small rapids before the waterfall; no big deal. But then we got to the eddy where we were all sitting waiting for our turn, and I see the tops of trees and a small mist rising from the pool below. My best friend Kenya was explaining the best way to run this waterfall and how to lean forward and tense up after five or so minutes; then he peeled out and I saw my best friend drop out of sight. I knew it was my turn to go and as I get to the lip, everything goes into slow motion. I have a feeling of euphoria as I take a big stroke and come off--not the cleanest, but I had done it. Once again, the feeling of being on top of the world overwhelmed me as I rushed to the take-out to hike back up and run it again. I had no nervousness or fear but I was naive and did not even think about that. After we ran the rapids again, we were back in the same position we were looking at treetops and mist. I was pushed to the left side of the lip and took no stroke as I feel the full 18 feet onto my head heard a terrible noise: the waterfall beating down on my kayak. I tried to roll up several times, but I could get no air. I let go of my paddle and I pulled my skirt. Now I am swimming and I'm not in my boat, but something was different. I was not getting air...but how could that be? All I can feel are little bubbles similar to what you feel when you drink soda; they were tickling my face. I tried to swim upwards, but I could not get to the surface. I saw light and I tried to take a breath but got nothing but water. At this point, I'm running out of air and I started to panic. I feel a large object smash into the back of my helmet. My kayak! I spun around and could only get one hand clutched onto a grab handle. My boat is floating away from me, away from the bottom of the waterfall that was trying to suck me under. My shoulder was being pulled so hard I expected it to get dislocated, but luckily the boat pulled me right out. Now I am on the surface, swimming in the pool. Each breath I take feels like I am being stabbed in the side over and over. I had broken two ribs but did not know it. It didn't seem like I was in there very long, but I was underwater with no air for 45 seconds, and your body will take an involuntary breath at 50 seconds. I had pushed my limit and the river had humbled me. Each time I go kayaking, I think about that day. I know the river demands respect and if you don't give it respect, it will ruin your day. Most people think that after that experience I should have quit kayaking, but that day showed me that no matter how good of a boater you are, you can always improve. I have made it my life goal to become a better kayaker and I still am on that path as I write this story.

I can still say there is no bad day on the river, and this sport has taken my life and changed it quite a bit. I used to hate the river and would not like going outside, but as soon as I started kayaking, it showed me a better quality of living than I could ever imagine. All I can think about now is where I will go next, what kind of people I will meet, and where my next step will take me. At the time that I am writing this, I am raising money to go along with scholarships I have gotten from WCKA (World Class Kayak Academy) so I can go finish my senior year in Chile and Colorado. I also plan on doing a North America kayaking tour where I start in North Carolina, go west to Colorado, up to Canada, back to the east, and come back to North Carolina through the east coast states while hitting some of the best whitewater in the world. After that, I plan on moving up into the Great Smoky Mountains and go to college and become a firefighter.

*****

Just Me and You by Daelin Duran

You and I are about to get really close. What you are reading is practically my entire life story and how I got from where I was back then to where I am today. I grew up in a small city called Little Rock, Arkansas, and when I say small, I mean VERY small. If you were to live there and leave your house to run some errands, you will most likely encounter a handful of people that you know by name. I was blessed to live near a very large portion of my family members, including both sets of grandparents. That was a blessing because they were there to make my childhood memorable, like taking me to the park and helping to raise me. I have two sisters Danielle and Kayla, who are older but not so much wiser. Danielle is ten years older than me and Kayla is five years older than me, so I am the baby and got plenty of wanted and unwanted attention. Which means I always got caught if I did anything wrong or I got rewarded when I did something good.

My mom stayed at home to watch my sisters and me, but would sometimes help my dad out in the little store he owned called Boot Hill (which sold western wear). Although we left Arkansas when I was two, I can still sing the full jingle for Boot Hill. My parents were very loving and spoiled us more than they should have. We moved quite a lot when I was young, a total of four times, if I'm not mistaken. All the moving was for the best, even if we didn't see it that way in the beginning. We packed up and left all my relatives in Arkansas and moved a few hours away to Tennessee. I don't remember much about Tennessee because I was still so young, but I do remember the house we were living in was huge. The trip from Arkansas to South Carolina is 17 hours, which is a big deal because we go back home at least four times a year. He moved our family to Fort Mill, South Carolina, where we would live in a tiny apartment until our house was finished. However, my dad did not stay there with us because he was already at our new house. It's crazy to me how I remember so much from that apartment when we didn't even stay there a full year. That apartment was where Kayla taught me how to swim and Danielle made me green eggs and ham. I shared a room with Kayla, so I'm surprised I lived through that, seeing how we fought all the time. One of my favorite memories was when my new pre-K teachers came to visit me and let me pick out a book and talk to them. The book was called *Just Me and You* and I scribbled my name and my age on the front cover to claim it. That book was my most prized possession, and my mom and I still quote it to this day. The quote we repeat is, "just me and you"-- it's what the little duckling says to her mom. Whenever they go anywhere, she asks, "Will it just be me and you?"

When we finally got to move into our house in York, South Carolina, we were all excited. It was a pretty big house and was in a neighborhood with a bunch of children my age. Danielle graduated from Clover High School and so did Kayla. I, however, did not get to stay in the Clover school district. In seventh grade my math teacher was fired for doing something inappropriate, so my mom sent me to Gaston Christian School. This is really when my life got flipped upside down, and I'm not sure why it happened. My eighth and ninth grade year went fine, however, I began to realize I was not like anyone at that school. Being in that school looked a lot like a *Teen Vogue* magazine. They were all really wealthy and looked like perfect Barbie dolls and no one was over a size four, except for me.

I started to feel the pressure and so did my parents. My mom had to get a job at Clover High School in the lunchroom to afford the school tuition and lifestyle. And I would beg and plead to get designer clothes and bags. But even when I did get those things for Christmas or my birthday, I still wasn't happy because I was still chubbier than all the pretty girls. I was so focused on looking like them that my grades started to fall and so did my spirit. I became very antisocial and rude to everyone, including my parents. My mom took me to our family doctor where I was diagnosed with ADD. The pills they gave me to cure me also made me feel full and not want to eat, which I was actually really excited about it because I started dropping a lot of weight and fitting in. But then the whole not eating that led to something I was not excited about and actually terrified of: I started having severe panic attacks. It's not like in the movies when some tiny, preppy, popular teenage girl is jumping up and down crying and fanning her face. No, this was more like curling into a ball and screaming or holding onto the sides of a toilet, never actually getting sick but only feeling better if I was beside it. It got to the point where I couldn't go to school for weeks.

My mom thought I was faking it until one day she looked in my eyes and said she could see the terror they held. She took me to work with her where I would sit in the lunch ladies breakroom and color. I couldn't even get in a car to go to the Walmart right up the road from my house. Every time my mom tried to take me somewhere she would have to turn around because I couldn't stop screaming, crying, or shaking. I missed two weeks of school before spring break and one week after. I went to every urgent care and family doctor, and no one knew what was setting these attacks off, even after testing me for everything in the book. Finally one night it got to the point my parents took me to the emergency room where more tests were taken and I had an IV in my arm the whole night giving me crazy amounts of fluid. Still they couldn't find an answer, so I was put on more medicine and sent home. My parents tried to find things to get my mind off of the pain, and that's where my horses come in.

Within walking distance of my house was a little horse ranch owned by this sweet old lady and her dad. As soon as we pulled up, I fell in love with every horse, goat, dog, cat, and chicken this lady owned. So my parents signed me up to take horseback riding lessons every Thursday after school. I started by just riding the most tame horse in circles over and over again. Then I started spending every weekend there mowing the fields, cleaning stalls, and breaking (also known as taming) some of the rowdier horses. I also went to my first competition and won each of the six categories I entered. Spending all that time there helped me almost fully overcome the panic attacks. It showed me no matter how big something is, I can have control over it. My parents finally took me out of Gaston Christian and put me in a very tiny school known as Blessed Hope.

The summer before I started my ninth grade year, I went to Trinidad and Tobago with my church group. That is where my life got completely changed around for the better. Going to places like those and seeing how truly blessed I was let me know my panic attacks are so small compared to what other people have to endure. For example, we were doing a roadside church service in a bad area in Trinidad, and my pastor's wife wanted us to walk from house to house asking locals to come out and join us. I must've passed at least four groups of people offering me drugs, and I overheard a couple screaming and hitting each other. Then I walked up to a house where my heart was stolen. It was a tiny house, probably just one room, with an outhouse in the back. I went up and before I could knock, a lady rushed out and handed me a five month old baby boy. She screamed, "Take my baby! I'll be back," and it shocked me to the point I just froze while holding this baby.

The guy I was walking with took my phone and took a picture that I still have today. After three hours of holding this baby tightly to my chest and watching carefully to make sure no one tried to harm the baby boy, the mother returned. She snapped a picture of me with him, then took him and went inside. They night made me realize just how much life is a treasure and how important every single person is. If I wasn't there to hold him, she would have given him to a different person who could've hurt him. When I returned home and started school, I had a positive outlook on everything and everyone. I loved Blessed Hope--even though some of the rules like uniform and only writing in pen were weird to me--and I learned more there than I have at any other school. But unfortunately the high school got shut down, so I had to find a new school and that's when I found York Preparatory Academy.

I love this school because it has taught me how to be strong and stand up for myself. Since starting York Prep, I also got two jobs. My first was working at TC's scooping ice cream and the other is being a cashier at Publix. Between school and work and overcoming my panic attacks, I feel like I'm ready to embrace the real world...which is a good thing, because I move out of my parents' house on May 14, 2016, to a little house with my best friend. As for college, I have decided it's not for me. I'm not a big fan of school and don't see wasting a bunch of money to sit in a class and stress about tests and then pay back a bunch of money for a degree I probably won't ever use. Publix has already offered to make me full time and I enjoy working and money so that is why I am choosing that route. So now that you know my past, plans for the future, and how important believing you can overcome your personal obstacles is, I hope you never fear the small things and have faith in yourself that you can overcome anything.

*****

Cutting into Life by Lauren Forsythe

"A good surgeon operates with his hand, not with his heart," said Alexandre Dumas. Being a surgeon is all about making few mistakes and doing what is best for the patient. Today, I removed a middle-aged woman's gallbladder. Open gallbladder removal is a fairly simple procedure, but there is always the possibility of complications. The patient could have an allergic reaction to the anesthesia, excessive bleeding, blood clots, damage to a blood vessel, infection, injury to the bile duct or small intestine, inflammation in the pancreas, etc. As a surgeon, I have to be prepared for all the possibilities and outcomes of the procedure. As I was scrubbing in, I watched the nurses prepare my patient for surgery. I asked my patient to count from one to ten and then ten to one, as I do with all my patients in the operating room. Before they finish counting to ten, they are normally out and ready to go. "Ten blade," I said. It was time for the incision. As I mentioned, there are always complications in surgery. My gallbladder patient had damage to one of her blood vessels. I had to perform an emergency angioplasty to repair her damaged blood vessel. As I am injecting the dye to start the procedure, I found a blockage in my patient's arteries. I had to insert a guidewire, then a balloon catheter. The balloon catheter inflates, taking in plaque from the wall of the artery. After the procedure, my care team closed the site where the catheter was inserted. Then my patient was stable, and the main incision was ready to be closed.

As I sewed up my patient's incision, I remembered how my mom used to sew me up with band aids on my scraped knee or elbow. The highest level of education my mom attained was two years at a technical college; as for my dad, he was a high school graduate, although, he did attain two years at a biblical college. With my parents not achieving a very high level of education, they've always told me how they wanted me to do better than they did. My parents always had confidence in me, but they thought it would be a challenge for me. I was adopted from birth. My birth mother was a cocaine addict and I was expected to have learning disabilities. The doctor told my mom I would be behind others in school and I would have reduced intelligence and social skills. He told her I would have deficits in some aspects of cognitive performance, information processing, and attention to tasks. My mom told me that I was never tested for learning disabilities immediately because she wasn't worried about it. She explained how the only thing she was worried about was her beautiful baby girl, and how that beautiful girl was all hers. Adoption is a very long and expensive process. After my mom went through hell to get me, she didn't want to worry about anything else; she was just happy to have me. As time went on, she told me I never showed any signs of having a learning disability, and my doctor agreed with her. My doctor told her that I was simply a blessing.

Growing up as a biracial child, my friends would always have numerous questions for me. It was hard for them to understand the whole adoption process. Sometimes, kids would ask me why both of my parents were white. Sometimes I would joke around and say that my mom cheated on my dad with a black guy and had me because that was easier for kids to understand, rather than the explanation of the whole adoption process. Being an adopted child, I would sometimes think of my birth mother. She never really crosses my mind nowadays and quite frankly, that is beneficial because I have to be completely focused in my OR. I have never met my birth mother but I have seen pictures of her. I never really had the intentions of meeting her, and still don't. Going through all of this, my mom had to adapt to some changes. My mom had no idea how to do my hair. There would be times where she would leave me looking like Corbin Bleu, have my hair in pigtails, or even attempt to braid it. It came to a point where we would be in stores, and my mom would ask random black women how to do my hair. My mom finally caught on to it, as did I. Even though my mom would leave my hair in a hot mess some days, I am so thankful she adopted me because I wouldn't be where I am today if it weren't for her.

My mom always pushed me to do better in school. She encouraged me to join a club or to compete in a sport. My mom was always really hard on me when it came to my grades. I was never allowed to have under a B average, and if I did, I got something I valued very much taken away from me. When I was in middle school, she would take my phone. When I was in high school, she would take my car keys. My mom never had to worry about taking anything from me much because I always maintained a B average or higher. In high school, and even middle school, she is the reason I was in advanced and honors courses. She is the reason I took dual enrollment and AP courses in high school. She is the reason I joined Beta Club and National Honors Society. She is the reason I got a full ride to Davidson College in North Carolina. She always pushed and encouraged me to do better and always told me that I could do it. She was right; I could do it.

I realized I wanted to be a surgeon when my brother broke my finger. I was in the seventh grade, and I remember it like it was just yesterday. Josh and I were playing soccer in the house. I never really knew much about soccer. I reached down to grab the ball, and at the same time, Josh kicked it, and broke my ring finger. My dad immediately took me to the urgent care, where they taped it up and scheduled me an appointment with a pediatric orthopedic surgeon three days later. Those three days couldn't have gone by any slower. On the day of the appointment, I had to have some x-rays done; my surgeon told my mom and I how he would need to take me into surgery to repair my finger. He had to insert three permanent screws into my finger, as well as a push pin, that was removed two weeks later. I loved how it all worked; it was fascinating. I loved everything about the hospital environment--everything from the cool blue scrubs to the blue caps the surgeons got to wear. I loved the mask, and especially the stethoscopes. I loved the thought of helping people. It was that day I realized I wanted to be a surgeon.

Now, here I am, the head of general surgeons, at Seattle Grace Hospital. I have performed more successful surgeries than bad. Tomorrow, I am scheduled to remove a ten year old boy's tonsils. This is supposed to be a very simple surgery and should go very well, but like I said, there are always complications in surgery. The surgery time will range anywhere from twenty to thirty minutes, without complications. After surgery, the patient has to take time to recover. Recovery is a process. It takes time. It takes patience. It takes everything you've got. As you're healing, you will develop a scar. My mom once told me, "From every wound there is a scar, and every scar tells a story, a story that says you survived." Just like the scar on my finger, the day I realized I wanted to be where I am today.

*****

Dear Freshman Me by Emma Gargiulo

"High school will be the best four years of your life... enjoy it while it lasts." I can't tell you how many times I've been told this. Every time I hear it, I can't help but think to myself that's a load of... let's say 'crap.' High school is full of drama, school work, responsibilities, and losses. It wasn't until the last semester of my senior year did I realize that it wasn't a load of crap at all; it's actually probably the truest thing I've ever heard. But let's start from the beginning.

Freshman year is gonna be great. You'll make the cheer team at Fort Mill, you'll break your hand but that's okay--your cast is pretty. The football games are great! The uniforms are ugly and look like tennis uniforms, but oh well, can't change that. Your grades are the best they've ever been, so keep it up! You're having a great year until about halfway through the year, when the troublemaker side really comes out. You have a tendency to speak when you shouldn't and you don't have much of a filter, which you'll learn to control later on. But you need to realize you can't fight other people's fights this year. When a boy on the bus pushes other girls too far, you decide to take matters into your own hands. It seems like a good idea to just deck him right in his jaw. He didn't touch a single girl again, but you get into serious trouble--even though I know we did the right thing. Mom was proud of you, and that's all that matters. The rest of your year goes pretty smooth--just typical "Emma" stuff here and there, but nothing crazy.

Now it's time for sophomore year! Finally you're no longer the underdog! You're back on the cheer team, and this time you're cheering with your best friend Sydney. Unfortunately, it's not as great as you think. All is good until about the time of your sweet 16. You and Syd start fighting, and in all honesty, I don't even remember why we started fighting in the first place--that's how stupid it was. You try to work things out but it's just never the same. One things leads to another, your temper takes over, and you get kicked off the team. You're devastated; you just give up. You start to get mixed up in the wrong crowd, partying every weekend, even on school nights. You think all these people you hang out with are your friends, but they aren't! You start to figure that out when you get arrested for being in the wrong place at the wrong time. You end up in the police station lying to the cops trying to protect those idiots. You cry and say you learned your lesson and you'll straighten up and stay out of trouble.. LIES! Soon enough, there's another fight and another experience with handcuffs. Have fun calling Mom about that one. You go through the arbitration system, do all your community service, but you also get court-ordered therapy, which starts in March. You like your therapist; she's really nice and helps you out a lot. Even after the court-ordered sessions expire, you decide to continue on in therapy. After a month, you finally told the whole story behind the scariest thing that has ever happened--when you were raped. It wasn't easy and you couldn't have done it without your support system of friends and family being there for you but after ten long, emotional years, you finally did it. It felt good, like there's a heavy weight lifted off your chest and you're able to breathe again. It leads to a lot of big decisions. It was like you got a fresh start. You got a tattoo and decided to change schools and decided to start over.

It's junior year, and you've started at YPA. It's nothing like Fort Mill; it's small and the people are completely different than those you're used to. You pretty much hate everyone because they aren't the people you've grown up with. You feel like you're constantly being judged, but you're use to knowing pretty much everybody and having tons of friends. Well, now it's your turn to be the new girl. You're quiet the first few months, and people are starting to accept you, but it still doesn't feel right. But then you become friends with someone who will eventually impact your life more than you know. Her name is Jordan. Y'all started out hating each other for no reason, but you're in the same group for spirit week and that's where it all began: the countless memories and crazy adventures and late nights and stupid decisions. You become best friends and eventually she becomes the most important person in your life; she keeps you in line in school and keeps you out of trouble.

After a great summer at the beach it's time for senior year. You don't really think much about college, just trying to get through the year. The year started out with an easy schedule and everything was great. You and Jordan will be working with Mom and Dad and a guy named Cory. Y'all started getting close over the summer time and then soon enough, you two become best friends. On December 1, Cory will drive home late at night and end up wrecking into a tree. Mom and Dad woke you up the next morning and had to tell you he passed away. You've buried friends before but nothing compares to how it was with Cory. You go visit his tree a lot and hang out with is little sister and eat dinner with his parents. It still doesn't seem real, but it's gotten easier.

You don't know what's going to happen over the next few months, but you've been through a lot and (hopefully) learned enough from those experiences to make good decisions. So have fun while you can and take every opportunity you get, because "High school will be the best four years of your life…so enjoy it while it lasts."

*****

Racing to the Finish Line by Hailey Hawkins

It's race day, the day that I always look forward to. I get to the track, take the car out of the trailer, get everything ready to run, all with the help of my dad, and then I stop and think about how I need to do my best and try to win the whole race. Racing isn't easy. I am constantly made fun of for driving a "rocketship." My car is long and kind of looks like a pencil. But I am also a girl who is more involved with cars than most boys are. Along with "rocketship," I am also teased with the words of "all you do is drive in straight line." The difference between drag racing and NASCAR racing is that in drag racing, we race in a straight 1/8 or 1/4 mile line, racing against one opponent at a time, while in NASCAR, you drive around in circles racing against forty other racers. These words just make me want to try even harder, and push myself to prove everyone wrong.

Even today, women who are in predominantly male-dominated industries are not common, and are not treated the same. However, it is becoming more common and more acceptable. Take the world of drag racing, for instance. Many years ago, women weren't even allowed to race; however, when Shirley Muldowney entered this male-dominated sport in 1958, she turned heads and changed the path for the rest of us women who would later on become a part of the sport as well. Shirley became the first woman to ever drag race, as well as the first woman to ever win, and although she was not treated the same in the sport, she turned the male-dominated sport into a sport where the men were "dominated" by her. Thanks to Shirley, today, over a quarter of all drag racers are girls.

I grew up at the race track. I was there almost every weekend possible with my dad, who raced for thirty years. My dad's racing career ended in May 2015. He was in a terrible accident; while going over 175 miles per hour, his motor blew up, engulfing the cockpit with flames. He was unable to see due to the fire, so he let go of the steering wheel and hit a telephone pole, causing the front end to be ripped off, and not a second after, causing him to flip four or five times in the air. Luckily, the car landed on the two back tires as they were the only two left on the car. Thankfully, a fellow racer, Teddy Houser, ran to my dad and reached into the car, still on fire, and pulled my dad out. My dad was badly burnt and spent over two months in Wake Forest Baptist Hospital in Winston-Salem, North Carolina. At first, we weren't sure if he was going to make it. He was on a ventilator for nineteen days, and had second to third degree burns on thirty percent of his body. His car was destroyed, and not much was left to be salvaged. There were a few times in the hospital when my dad said that he didn't want my sister, who also races, or me to race anymore. Later on, he changed his mind about that because he knew we loved racing and didn't want that to be taken away from us, like it had just been for him. Seeing my dad experience all of the pain he was having did make me think. Every one of us who races, and puts ourselves in a race car, knows that something bad happening is always a possibility, no matter if you think it will happen to you or not. That is just a part of the sport. I know the things that could happen, but I still want to race. By continuing to race, I know I am taking a risk, but it's something I love to do. It's what I grew up around. I don't know if I could live without it--without the thrill or the joy that I get from it. It has been almost a year since my dad's crash, and he is still healing from that awful, unforgettable day. I am more than thankful to God for sparing my dad's life. It just wasn't his time to go, and God knew that we would need him. This day changed my family's life forever.

I've got many plans for the steps that I take next in life. With one year of high school left, things are starting to approach very fast. In my future, I plan on attending college at Winthrop University and I will major in Interior Design. I plan on continuing with my drag racing career and creating a family once I am settled down and have created a life for myself.

When I pull up to the line in my car, many things start running through my mind. I start thinking about how I want to make my dad and sponsors proud. If I were to put things in perspective, thinking while in the driver's seat is a lot like thinking about what I want to do in my future. For instance, my life right now, is basically the same as if I were sitting in the driver's seat. My parents still have a lot to do with how I am going to plan my future. They are still teaching me values, and are always trying to help me lead my life in the greatest way possible. My parents are along for the ride, but I am the one that is driving my way to my career and my future. I am paving my path to a new part of my life.

*****

Scout's Honor by Landon Hoffman

Throughout my life thus far, I can say the main skill I have learned is work ethic. My parents instilled in me this value from when I was young. For me, it has always been about the plan to be successful. I know that success isn't measured money or fame, however, it is an outcome I'm striving to achieve along with being content. The steps I've taken thus far are to prepare me for challenges and obstacles that may stand in the way of true success.

When I was in kindergarten, my older brother was in the first grade and he joined the Cub Scouts. I can still recall how amazing the program seemed, and I could not wait to be old enough to be a part of this challenging program, where activities like camping and competition activities were unlimited. My parents and Scoutmasters always spoke of what a great honor it was if you stayed in Scouts and achieved the rank of an Eagle Scout.

I continued through Cub Scouts until the fifth grade, when I bridged in the program and became a Boy Scout. This is when I really became excited about scouts, because I enjoyed working in fast-paced environments. I liked Boy Scouts better for many reasons, but mainly to self-pace my projects. In Cub Scouts, we did everything as a group and each school year we would advance a rank, if we had completed all the requirements. This was great when I was younger, but I was soon ready to go like a racehorse in the starting gate. I have always been the type of person who wants do everything as fast as possible and excel.

In the sixth grade, I started Boy Scouts and hit the ground running. I was so ready and excited for summer camp. This was an opportunity for me to earn lots of merit badges and do fun activities. I remember it was fun, but I also wished that I had taken some other more fun classes, rather than just listening to my brother who said that I needed to take some Eagle required badges, rather than just purely fun classes. The badges I really wanted to take were canoeing, woodcarving, and archery. There are twenty-one merit badges required to earn the rank of an Eagle, from first aid to financial management. My brother persuaded me to take some not-as-fun badges, such as emergency preparedness and environmental science, due to them being Eagle-required. In the end, I'm glad I listened because it helped me immensely.

I worked proficiently and thoroughly through Scouts. When I hit the age of fourteen, I had almost everything I needed to start my Eagle Scout project, which involved renovating a room for my church's ministry center that distributes clothes and households items to those less fortunate in our community. I built strong racks and a shelving system that would make it easier to sort and prepare the donated items. I had to fundraise the money and organize help to complete the project.

That summer I did so and stuck with Scouts and later that summer it was finally time for my Board of Review with the official Eagle Board. I was so nervous; I couldn't sit still. I remembered entering the room where I would be quizzed and asked about anything and everything throughout my scouting career. As soon as I walked in, I saw four men look at me with a puzzled look on their faces. The first question I was asked was, "Son, how old are you?" I replied back in a nervous trembling voice, "I'm fourteen, sir." The four men then continued to quiz me with what I learned, and some more specific questions such as, "What are the five signs of a heart attack?", as well as others. Then the time came for me to leave the room. I stepped out for them to deliberate on whether they thought I was worthy of the rank of an Eagle Scout. They called me back in and congratulated me on passing the review and for being the youngest scout they had seen in "quite a long time" to achieve Eagle. The scouting program taught me that everything is not just purely fun. You have to take the opportunities when they come and buckle down and get it done; stick with it and get through.

When I was ten, my dad began cutting my grandmother's grass. Just like any other kid, I wanted to go with my dad and help. He always gave me the job of picking up sticks, so the lawnmower would not hit them and damage the blades. He paid me $5 every time we went, and I continued to go for about two years, always doing the same thing. I continuously begged him to let me cut some grass or use the weed-eater, but I always received the same answer: "No." He finally came around to letting me blow the driveways off, and by this time, my grandmother's neighbors had asked us to begin cutting their yards also, so we quoted a price and began cutting. I soon started running the mower, which was what I thought to be a fancy one, because it was a zero turn. I fell in love with it and began cutting the grass at my house every weekend, teaching myself how to stripe and perfecting how straight my lines were. I must say, at the age of thirteen I was pretty dang good. We called our business HLC for "Hoffman Lawn Care." Without any effort, we started gaining more customers. We soon had about ten clients and needed new equipment to keep up with our frequent use. We budgeted and bought the necessary equipment. After ninth grade, I figured it was time for a real summer job. I requested a meeting with a family friend who owned his own lawn care business, and he offered me a job. I worked my butt off that summer, four days a week, ten hours a day, but the paychecks made it worthwhile. On my days off, I still cut my personal yards with my dad and brother for our business. I learned the hard way sometimes, like learning to stick with it when I would do something wrong and get fussed at by my crew leader. Most importantly, I learned to stick with it and get through.

I am currently a junior and looking forward to the future. In order to graduate high school next year, I only have to take one class, so I will have lots of free time. I wish to enroll at York Tech and take classes there to help me get ahead. I will obtain a two year certificate from York Technical College in electronics and then go straight to work for Duke Energy and become a Service Tech. I chose this career because it involves being outside and I won't have a boss over my shoulder at every moment throughout the day. Duke Energy is a large company that brings its own benefits, and the industry will be around or a long time. The job I want is also one that cannot be replaced with a robot or anything of that nature which is good for job security. I'm going to stick with the task at hand, and persevere through any obstacles I might encounter.

I have never been one to get caught up in fancy cars and houses or anything of that nature. I like the simple things in life, such as hanging out with friends and playing sports. Even though I am young, I still see the big picture for myself and the next step to take. My work ethic will aid me in making a difference in the workforce and also the schooling it requires to get there.

*****

The Game of Life by Kelsey Hudson

Imagine you are playing a game and you can't win for anything. You and your friends keep playing and they are enjoying this game, but you lose over and over again. That is how I feel every day. In this game of life, I feel like I am on the losing end. Yes, I have friends, but how do you meet new people and decide if they will be the ones you trust with your secrets?

When I was eight, I wasn't aware of how much my life was about to change. My mother started to leave at night and walk to the bar. I would watch her out of my window and be so confused: where she was going? What she was doing? Then I wondered why my dad stopped fighting for her to stay. My dad would leave for work at night and I would see random men in my house who weren't my dad. For a while, I had to cook dinner for my brother and sister and help them get ready for bed, even though I didn't know how to take care of myself, let alone two smaller kids. One day I came home and my dad was awake, which was unusual because he works third shift. My mother was sitting with him on the porch. He asked all of us to come "talk." We sat and saw tears running down both of their faces, and as we watch the awkwardness of who would be the one to tell us the saddest line of our lives. We were silent. My dad explained how he loved us and wanted us to know that, while our mom sat silent. I looked at my brother and sister and they didn't understand. I knew more about the situation than they did, but even I was confused. My unspoken question was, "How do parents choose to not love their children anymore?" My dad left my mom, but I don't blame him because she was a raging alcoholic, a cheater, and a liar. I know people are human and they make mistakes, but you should never stop loving your kids, and you should never respect the bottle more than your husband. Do I hate my mother? No, but she is someone I lost.

After my parents' divorce, things went downhill. Our house was foreclosed, my dad started renting an apartment and my mom started "dating." She met a man named Lance Awbrey, who was a lot younger than she was and he still lived with his parents. That's not always a bad thing, but it added to my aggression. He had a really nice car and a good paying job. His parents were great people and took us in as their own grandchildren. After a year of living with his parents, they got an apartment and we moved again. It made me hate him worse; I can't tell you why I hated him so much other than the fact that I hated my mom and to see her happy was fueling the fire. I had no control over being with her, either; my dad worked third shift and we only got to see him on the weekends. Looking back now, I know Lance was a great man--he took in three kids who weren't his own and loved them. We had some great times together, but they were few and far between. I would fight him and disobey because I wanted him out of my life. I regret that so much now. I wish I could go back, realize what a huge aspect he would play in my life, and cherish the small things. In 2012, he and my mom got engaged, but then she cheated on him, and it wrecked him. He took his own life a few months later. Lance is also someone I lost.

After Lance's death, we moved back to my dad's house. Shortly after, he started seeing a woman named Mary Little. We fought and didn't always get along, but I loved her. She treated my family and me like her own, and her past wasn't too far off from ours. She had two kids, Ethan and Kannon. Mary and my dad married in April 2014, and she became my mother. However, on September 25, I woke up and could hear her alarm blaring. It was weird to still hear her alarm, but I ignored it and went back to my room to get ready for school. A few minutes later, my sister came into my room and asked me to go checked on Mary. I looked at her funny and said, "Why are you so scared? It isn't like she is dead." I will regret that forever, because when I went to her room to check on her, something didn't feel right. Her sons followed me in there and so did my sister. I went to touch her and her body was cold. I tried to shake her and couldn't get her up. I yelled for my sister to turn the alarm off and told the boys to finish getting ready. I called 911 and my sister called my dad. I remember the EMS asking where my dad was, so I gave him the phone. I handled it the best I could, but she was gone. Five months after making a family, she passed away from a seizure in her sleep. I broke down; I cried and I was pissed. Everyone was crying and that's all I choose to remember day. She meant so much to my family; she showed me how to be a young woman and right from wrong. I miss her every day. She is also someone I lost.

After the loss, I gained nothing. I felt empty. How can you build relationships when you are afraid of losing? How do you go back onto the field after halftime to finish a game when the score is 20 to 0? I couldn't, and after all that loss, I began to lose myself. I lost it drinking and partying with friends. I lost it in sleeping and crying and not wanting to speak. I found myself at my lowest. I was failing in school--I knew I could do better, but couldn't make myself. Every day I'd wake up and be angry and hateful. I never realized how much I still had, only how much I had lost. I felt alone and hurt.

One day I got a Facebook message from my softball coach. She asked how I was doing and if I wanted to go get some Starbucks, and that is the day my life changed. I spent the night with her and her family of two daughters, son, and grandson. The more time I spent with Heather, the more my family would want to. Before long, my brother befriended her son. I think my sister and my dad were more skeptical, which is understandable on both sides. Both of our families had gone through a lot the last couple of years and we all wanted to be happy. After a few weeks of my siblings and I hanging out with Heather, she started dating my dad. Heather and Garrett moved into my dad's home. Now that I have lived with Heather and her family and we have created a life, I feel like I have a future; I feel like our families have a future. We are creating new memories, new bonds, as ONE new family. We are not perfect and probably never will be, but we are perfect for each other! They are the family I gained.

There is no doubt that my life has been sad and full of loss, but my father always tells me, "Do NOT allow your past to change your future." I have a sense of purpose. Not just because I live with Heather and her son, but because I can see that happiness isn't about everyone else. Happiness is about finding yourself and letting the world see that. I am not proud of my past, but I am proud of the person it has made me. So in this "Game of Life" I will continue playing--I will have losses, but I will also be a winner.

*****

It's Not Me, It's You by Rosie James

Dear SAT:
Before you came along, I struggled. Before I had even seen you, people praised you. I was told we would be a perfect fit. All my life I have heard of people who get into relationships and are not happy, but they do not leave, but

I never understood why. And yet, here I was debasing myself to please you, who pretended to have my best interest at heart. I know we were not together for very long, but it felt like a lifetime. Immediately, I trusted you and let you overwhelm my mind. Why not? Everybody else trusted you. You were everything I thought about. I worked to keep you happy. I believed you were what I needed. I believed that you would help me, be there for me. I tried everything you told me to. I dressed up for you. I dressed down for you. I bought new things for you. I gave up friends for you.

Believe me, in my eighteen years, I have made a lot of bad associations, trusted a lot of things, but not one of them has torn me down like you. I based my intelligence and self-esteem on you. I let you influence my self-worth. I signed a part of myself over to you, not seeing your impossible standards in the fine print. I realize now that I should not have placed this in your hands. But now it is too late, I can never be who I was before.

I used to be able to hold my head high. I used to be so proud of you--of us. My mom still loves you. My dad still loves you. Even my teachers still love you. They are blinded not seeing what you are—not seeing you the way I now can. They cannot see what you have done to me. They do not know how you manipulated me, how you contorted me until I no longer recognized my reflection, because I kept it inside, afraid of judgement.

You beat me up. You scarred me, left me bruised and battered. You left your mark so that I could never forget that we were together, so I could never pretend this was just a dream.

You knew how much I struggled when we first met. I told you how I have struggled with my self-worth. I told you how my education was hard-fought. You took my lifelong struggles, targeted every weakness, and used them against me.

I spent too many days studying you, trying to learn your patterns and behaviors, trying to figure out how to please you. I read page after page, literally memorizing your every nuance. I spent hours wondering how I world measure up, wondering if I had done enough, wondering what my future would be like with you. I consulted my friends on the matter. They tried to help me mend our relationship. They tried to help me please you. I called them in tears, and they consoled me. I did not realize then that I was not the problem.

You killed my spirit, labeled me insignificant—not good enough. I was nothing to you but a slave that you can manipulate, control. I wanted to leave. I begged to leave. Your threats and manipulation kept me in bondage. You told me I would be nothing without you. You told me I could not succeed without you. I believed you. At every encounter, you pushed me deeper and deeper inside myself, and I had to work harder and harder to try to gain your approval, approval that world never come.

Now, I say: ENOUGH! I will not let you tell me I am not worth anything. I will not let you say I am ignorant. I know that I am smarter than you will ever give me credit for. I will not let you tear me down. I know now that you do not define my life. I know now that you only defined these things because I let you.

I will not let you define my life. I will not let you determine my future, and I will not let you dictate my intelligence. I determine what I will do with my life. I choose what I will do with my future, and I will dictate my intelligence. My life is unique; I will not be labeled and defined as a number, by a machine. So, goodbye SAT. We are done, and you and I are through. I am done obsessing over you. I know my struggles, and I know how far I have come. I know that you grade everybody on a set scale, indeterminate of circumstances or struggle. I have become a different person because of you. It has taken some time to come to the realization that part of what you said is correct: I did need you to succeed. Without you, it would have taken me longer to see how strong I can be on my own. Without you, I do not know if I would have learned to love myself and my flaws.

I have spent years searching for approval. I have spent hours preparing for a test that would not see who I was. I do not need a test to define me. Goodbye. It's not me, it's you.

*****

The Exceptional Student by Jared A. Key

It has always been a struggle for me to learn and comprehend things as well as others. I found out that I had not one but two learning disabilities when I was in the fifth grade. At the time, I didn't fully understand what these disabilities were or how they affected my learning. The two learning disabilities that I was found to have are dyslexia and dysgraphia. These two disabilities have made it a serious challenge to get good grades in a lot of my classes, especially classes like English, history, and some science courses. Although they may affect my learning capabilities, they do not affect my stubbornness and desire to succeed. Even though I have trouble with English and history, I am really good at mathematics and some of the hands-on sciences courses. I have always loved working with my hands and creating new things. Therefore, I have decided to become a welder after I graduate high school. Being a welder would be perfect for me because I can create new things without my disabilities really affecting me. I plan on achieving this by going to a local tech college for a few years to get my degree.

My disabilities are mostly focused around reading, reading comprehension, and writing. Dyslexia is hard to explain. "A good way to understand dyslexia is to establish what it is not. It's not a sign of low intelligence or laziness. It's also not due to poor vision. It's a common condition that affects the way the brain processes written and spoken language...Dyslexia doesn't just affect reading and writing. It also affects certain everyday skills and activities such as social skills, listening comprehension, memory, navigation, and time management."[1] Dyslexia has really affected me throughout my life. There were times where it was had to learn because I would get distracted from my work and couldn't concentrate. There were other times when I'd try to read a story or a page out of my textbook and when I finished I couldn't remember what I read.

My other disability is called dysgraphia, "a condition that causes trouble with written expression. The term comes from the greek words *dys* ('impaired') and *graphia* ('making letter forms by hand'). Dysgraphia is a brain-based issue. It's not a result of laziness or low intelligence...For many kids with dysgraphia, just holding a pencil and organizing letters on a line is difficult. The handwriting tends to be messy."[2] There were a few teachers who really made me feel bad because they would always talk about how bad my handwriting was. This really hurt me sometimes because I knew that I couldn't help it because of my dysgraphia. Although these disabilities can make it extremely hard to pass and get good grades in school, it is not impossible.

Being a kid with these disabilities was pretty challenging with all the reading and work without fully understanding my disabilities. Growing up I never really understood my disabilities as well as I could have. I always tried to tell myself that there's was nothing wrong with me and that I was just like everyone else. But as time went on and I got older, the work got harder, which also made it much harder to hide the fact that I had these disabilities and that I needed help.

When I first found out about my disabilities I didn't really understand them. This made it hard for me to accept the fact that had these disabilities. I always thought, "Why me?" I always thought that I did something wrong. So this led me to think that I was stupid and I always expected to fail at everything. This really affected me because I just stopped trying. I thought, why even try if I was just going to fail?

After a while with the help of some close friends and some other significant people in my life, I came to realize that these disabilities were not really all that bad. They definitely don't make anything easier, but with time I've come

---

[1] Lapkin, Emily. "Understanding Dyslexia." Understood.org. 2 Apr. 2014. Web. 15 Dec. 2015.

[2] Patino, Erica. "Understanding Dysgraphia." Understood.org. 15 June 2014. Web. 16 Dec. 2015.

to accept the fact that I have these disabilities. Although it was hard to adjust, it was definitely not impossible.

After a while I've come to realize that having these disabilities isn't all bad. I get printed notes at school. They make math a lot easier by being able to move around numbers in your head. Another advantage is people with dyslexia tend to be very creative and are able to think outside the box. This makes life a lot more interesting. Being creative and thinking out of the box tends to lead to a good time. For example, when I was younger I used to love the arcade game skee ball. I loved this game so much I had an idea to make my own so I did. It was a challenge, but in the end I had a great time, which leads me back to welding.

To me, welding is a very attractive career, because it has always been something that has interested me. There are endless possibilities when it comes to what you can do with welding. You can do anything from making cool sculptures to home projects like fixing a handrail or building a frame for something. Welding is a two year course and it is a demanding career and just an overall great skill to have.

So as I reflect on my past and think about my future, I know my disabilities will have an impact on whatever I do. But now I know that I can get through it. It will be hard but nothing's impossible if you put your mind to it.

*****

Building My Future by John LeBrun

My life has never been a linear path; between athletics, academics, and moving away, most people would say it has been a wild ride. I came to York Preparatory Academy as a junior and it was a gigantic leap from my old school. The people are friendly and class rank isn't what students live for. This has allowed me to further my education without limits. The best thing about York Prep is the teachers. They are unlike any other teacher group I have ever had. The teachers work with you to understand advanced concepts that are upper college level and they try and prepare you for the college experience. This helps me as a student because if they prepare me now, then I have a high chance of succeeding in college when I get there. My high school experience has been busy but worthwhile, and I hope my college experience is just like it.

My high school life has been busy since I was a freshman. Never in my life have I had so little free time to do what I want to do--between school and extracurricular activities, I am a rare sight at home for anything other than sleep. This puts a lot of pressure on me to get my work done in a limited amount of time. I had prior commitments in my previous town that I was still required to do. I say 'required,' but I really mean I was obligated to stay with these commitments because nobody else would. Before I left Greenville, I was team captain of both the wrestling and robotics team so leaving was hard, but leaving the teams without leadership was even harder. The wrestling team was not an issue since I knew the capabilities of the people on it and finding a leader took no time, but the robotics team was a different story. Several people applied for team captain, but out of all the candidates, I was selected for some crazy reason, and then I had to make the choice of leaving everything behind or fulfill my duty as the elected official. I made the choice to commute back and forth to Greenville every day to be part of the robotics team. This commute to Greenville has had a huge impact on my school life since I don't get home until 10:00 pm each night. I have to balance when I can do school work and how much time I have for school projects. It was rough in the first semester, but I started getting used to it by the second semester. Robotics overall helped me to find the balance between school work and outside work and kept me going toward my goals.

The next step in my life is to go to college. I want to go to Annapolis or West Point, and hopefully I'm not shooting too high. A military academy has always been something that has interested me because they give a sense of unity and family that no other college could give. You form a tight bond with your fellow cadets and you become more than just roommates but brothers. This also ties in with me wanting to serve my country in the armed forces somehow. My grandfather was in the army and it set him on a path to go back to college and get a degree in law. If military leadership can inspire someone to go to college, then I want to see what it can do for me. I also want to join the military to push myself to greater limits, test my instincts, and overcome my weaknesses. I have a general idea that I want to major in political science but I haven't looked into that many jobs in that career cluster. I know I want a government job because they are pretty stable jobs and they provide benefits that few companies offer. I would also like to work with other countries in foreign affairs, such as a diplomat or in an embassy because I don't want to be just another guy watching the tv and thinking I could do better, I want to be the guy who makes the changes.

When most people think of a job, they first ask how much it pays then the hours you have to work. I want to know if I will truly enjoy going to work every day. If you step back and look at a job, money should not be an issue, because smart saving and investing can get you any salary you want, but if you truly look at a job you have to think about you spending up to forty years doing the same thing (or close to it). Is this the kind of work you want to do in the job field you want to be in? I hope to answer this question when I get out of college because I want to wake up and love going to my job. I want to learn new things that help me to explore higher education. I want to feel like I did something in college other than study and party; I want to become something different after college because of the experiences I had and the knowledge I gained. I want a job that helps a large group of people through my actions and makes me a better person. I want my life to be simple but impactful; I want to push someone to make the right choice.

My mentors are the people I look up to and strive to be like. They are the reason I am where I am today, they are the most important influence in my life, and they still keep me going today. Some of these mentors have given me life skills or helped me to get closer to my goals in life such as a man named Ray Cox; he gave me ninety percent of all my work based skills that I have today. He taught me how to problem solve and inquire knowledge by asking the right questions at the right time. In the short two years that he was my teacher, he passed on more knowledge than any other teacher in my life. Nothing was foreign to Mr. Cox, from engineering to art he was on top of teaching advanced ideas to third and fourth graders. He was also the first person to introduce me to the FIRST program (For Inspiration and Recognition of Science and Technology) which is a STEM (Science, Technology, Engineering and Math) based program that promotes and inspires young engineers through different robotic programs. FIRST brought me into contact with almost all my other mentors in my life throughout the years.

When I met Mr. Cox in third grade, he opened my mind to the idea of higher education. He stayed with me through fifth grade and then I went to Beck Academy Middle School and met Mr. Kimbrell. He kept me on the path of robotics but with a different outlook on things. He gave me hands-on experience of what engineers have to do to accomplish tasks; he would give us jobs to do and we had to draw blueprints, construct the project and then redesign it if it could be done more efficiently. On top of all that he only gave us three weeks. It was a grueling class but in the end it helped get people motivated and built a strong work ethic. My time in middle school helped me to build good characteristics but it took me away from the source of all my hard work which was FIRST. High school started and I was selected to join something called FIRST Robotic Challenge, or FRC for short. FRC was something completely different than what I was doing before. Instead of small challenges that I was given, it was forty students all working on a 120 pound robot that had to shoot yoga sized balls into a goal seven feet off the ground. This was a shock at first, but once I got into the swing of things, I met real engineers who taught the students so that they could build this robot. These people knew how to teach the idea, not to just do it themselves. They engaged us and pushed us to allow us to innovate and solve the problems ourselves. After a year of being under an electrical engineer, I was selected as the electrical sub-team captain, and then from showing more ability to lead, they thought I had what it takes to lead the whole team. The mentors really help me along the way by keeping me on task and pushing ideas that students come up with. The mentors didn't just influence the students through robotics, but also in college choices. They help you look through different colleges and find the best one for you. They also inspire the students to come back after college and mentor the team, repeating the process.

Sometimes when I try to think of what I want from life, my mind goes blank because I don't know if what I want now is what I will want in thirty years. I want to gain knowledge and wealth but those are every man's dream. What makes me different from the average man has not shown itself yet and that frightens me, for one day it will show itself whether or not I am ready for it. With all my heart I believe that FIRST is the only reason I work hard in school work and I still think they will have some sort of impact in my adult years. I want to gain things from high school and college, but most importantly, I want to become the mentor one day and help a student rise the ranks and want to become something. I guess that is my overall goal: to reverse the roles and become the mentor to make a child take the next step.

*****

It's Written All Over You by Nia Lindsay

"Nia, you're going to do something great. Your future is exceptionally bright. You're going to create milestones that exceed EVERYTHING your father and I have ever done. God has done, and will continue to do, marvelous works in your life. You are success. Success is you. It's written all over you."

Before any sports game, whether it be for a little league baseball team, or an all-star champion NFL team, players must make sure that they are physically prepared for the upcoming event. This includes daily practicing, stretching, and training. Although physical training is a key factor in determining whether the players are prepared, nothing is more important than the MENTAL preparation. This is the responsibility of the coach, the team members, and each individual to speak positivity and integrity for inner self-esteem and confidence. Even if a team member is feeling defeated, these mental "words of wisdom" will encourage bravery and allow the player to face the challenges and adversities ahead of them. My mother has always helped me with openly accepting and internalizing this positivity and self-confidence.

It is extremely common for people to question their true "purpose" in life...trust me, I know. From my personal experiences, it may seem as if I am on a never-ending quest filled with exploration, realization, and flat-out confusion. As this journey continues though, it is best to keep in mind that I do have a purpose in this world. A purpose that is customized, and made just for me. Coincidentally, my name is Nia, which literally means "purpose." Now I know what you're thinking: *"Oh, the irony!"* Believe it or not, the name has multiple origins; for example, "Nia" is also a variant of the Irish name, "Niamh", meaning 'bright.' However, the Swahili origin of the name meaning 'purpose' stands out to me the most. My mother has always explained to me, even as a little girl, how she had various name ideas for me. From the name "Love" (with no last name, just the first name "Love") to the name "Imani"(I'm assuming that would've included a last name, but was not chosen because of the word "enemy" sounding very similar to the name if said backwards), many names crossed her mind. However, "Nia" was the name chosen, which is a daily reminder that I have a purpose to fulfill.

Growing up, singing has always been a passion of mine and always will be. So much so that my preschool teachers were able to discern if I had a good day at school or not. "Nia wasn't singing today during reading time, is everything alright? Is she a bit 'under the weather'?" Or they would say something along the lines of, "Nia had a great day, singing and all!" I would perform multiple songs as I stood tall on my bed with a brush in hand as my stuffed animals and dolls would sit on the floor, "admiring" my voice. I guess you can already assume what I wanted my first occupational position to be. Although singing is a very important role in my life, reality hit me in about third grade. The music industry is pretty difficult to enter, and was not the career I wanted to major in or pursue as a lifetime career. From there, I agreed to continue singing, and consider it as a loved hobby. As I got older, I began to lean more towards helping people, specifically children. I loved the thought of assisting people in need, and there are a plethora of careers with that quality. I began to show more interest for pediatrics. Knowing that I could be with children while making them feel better was a "win-win" situation for me. I remember having a career project in class where we had to make a briefcase filled with things our specific jobs would require in that place of work. Some children said firemen, some said police officers; there were even a few ballerinas and chefs.

All of the boxes were interesting (as interesting as third graders could make it, of course), each of them filled with different things, some more than others. Now, being that I had an extremely creative mother, it would be most fitting that I was the kid with the "bells and whistles" project. I remember my suitcase vividly: four blue sanitation latex gloves surrounding the box blown up to have a realistic balloon shape. The word **'PEDIATRICIAN'** written in the center of the box, with big bright letters and small pictures outlining it. When it was my turn to present, I proudly stood in front of my eager classmates knowing that they were interested to see what was inside. I cleared my throat and with no hesitation, said, "I WOULD LIKE TO BE A BABY DOCTOR." Not realizing the obviousness of the statement I had just made, I began with my presentation excitedly showing little knick-knacks I put inside the box. From Band-Aids and stickers, to a stethoscope and a miniature cough syrup bottle, I described every item in the bag. Now that I think of it, my over-enthusiasm was probably a bit annoying, but it certainly didn't matter to me. To this day, I'm still considering pediatrics. I still love kids, and still enjoy being an aid for whoever needs immediate attention.

In the ninth grade, my career changed once again and leaned towards Psychology. Aside from loving to be of assistance physically, I also love being of assistance mentally as well. Towards the beginning of high school, I realized how easy it was to make friends. I have never met a stranger, and accept everyone for who they are. I also realized that most of my friends would come to me if they ever needed advice, or simply someone to talk to. I thought of this as a good thing because I knew this meant my friends trusted me and valued my opinion. I still have many friends who come to me for ideas and thoughts. I know that if I go in the field of Psychology, this aspect would continue to grow. Having someone come to you for a "shoulder to lean on" is always an honorable feeling.

I've been thinking of a couple of other majors and occupations as well, like law and event planning. I have (especially in my mother's opinion) the analytical, public speaking, and interpersonal skills to be in the field of law. I also enjoy being in charge of events. By no means is it easy, but seeing the finished product and observing how great everything comes together is a wonderful feeling. Truth is, I have no clue what I'm going to do in the future. One could say that my choice of future careers is completely uniquely different from each other in many different ways. However, they all have something in common. They all represent a part of me. They're all small pieces of my personality and characteristics.

One thing that I've learned about finding your "purpose" is that it's not easy. In fact, it may be one of the most difficult journeys in your life. But the relief of this is that not knowing your destiny is okay. In the end, it is a true blessing to know that God has a wonderfully ordained plan for everyone. Right now, my plan is to finish high school successfully and get accepted into a college that has the perfect stepping stones for my future. Like everyone, I have certain preferences and choices that stand out to me, however I know that if it is meant to be, it will be. Internal questions about my future are brought up in my head pretty much all of the time. Who wouldn't? However, I am sure to fulfill my mom's "words of wisdom:" my hopes and dreams, and my purpose.

*****

My Garden by Madi Mott

Every person has a garden. You can't see it because it's on the inside, but it's there. Everyone has flowers blooming inside of them. Depending on how a person nurtures their garden, those flowers can flourish and live on for years, or those flowers can die and a person has to live with an empty garden. Of course, other people can plant flowers in other gardens. They can be nice, compliment the person, and/or help a person out, and it may add flowers to that person's garden. Sometimes, people don't have any respect for other people's gardens. Some people go stomping through another's garden, smash all of the flowers to the ground, and leave ugly weeds in place of those beautiful flowers that they ripped out. Those weeds can stick around for a while, too. They're baneful; a person really has to try to eradicate those weeds. Sometimes a person never truly gets rid of the weeds. The roots are still there in the soil, and every once in a while, they'll rear their ugly heads as a reminder of what once happened.

My garden was stomped on this past year. It was destroyed by someone who didn't have the capacity to understand that what he was doing was going to ruin my garden for a long time. He ripped out my flowers and left such awful, ugly weeds. For a while, I didn't even care for my garden. I let the weeds grow and make a home there. I let this person come back, thinking that he was going to take the weeds out and plant the flowers that I wanted so badly. That didn't happen. Instead, he planted more weeds and even put boulders in my garden for me to trip over and fall to the ground. My garden was a mess and I didn't know how to fix it. Other people could see that my garden was beyond repair, or so everybody thought. People would try to help me; they would try to pull up some weeds and plant flowers, but it never worked. Weeds often overpower flowers. They take the nutrients out of the ground, away from the flowers' roots. It didn't look like there was any hope for my garden.

Then one day, the sun poked out from behind those gloomy clouds that hovered within me, and I saw the truly terrible shape that my garden was in. I knew it was going to take perseverance, but I decided I was going to fix my garden. I spent weeks ripping countless weeds out of my garden. It took me months to drag those boulders out. I had tremendous help from my closest friends. If I hadn't had their help, I don't think I could have ever dragged those boulders out. After my garden was cleared out, I knew I had to start from scratch. I planted one flower at a time, very carefully. I had to make sure I was doing this right; I didn't want to mess up. There were some days when I stopped. I didn't have the strength to plant and nurture delicate flowers in nutrient-lacking soil. But the next day I felt like I could, I planted another flower and tended it carefully.

I was cautious when I planted flowers and who I let around my garden; some people pick flowers because they think them to be pretty, but then they forget that they can't put that flower back. I had some people do that to my garden. They picked my flowers because it was easier to take mine than it was to plant their own in their garden. It was okay, though. I'd just plant the flower again. I put a fence up around my garden just to be safe. I relied on other people to also look after my garden and to make sure that nobody was going to come and pick at or stomp on my garden. With persistence, my garden began to grow.

My garden is beginning to bloom now. There are still some days when those clouds come rolling back in. Some days, stubborn weeds sprout back up in my garden, so I have to keep on a constant look out for them. After all, you can't just leave a garden to tend to itself. I still plant flowers because some flowers die if the conditions aren't right. If the season changes, if they don't get the right amount of sunlight, or if the flowers don't get watered enough, they can die. But I just pick those out and place new ones in their place. I know now that just because flowers die doesn't mean they aren't worth planting. So that is why I will continue to plant flowers. Roses may once again bloom in my garden; they have awful thorns, but I believe the right person will make them worth the pain. I will plant a tree one day, preferably a willow tree, and that tree will be placed at the center of my garden. I will plant it with the help of someone, and from that point on, he will always be there to help me look after my garden, and I will help him look after his.

In the future, I'd like to help people become aware of their own gardens because some people don't even realize they have one until it's smashed to the ground. Everyone should know about the garden, know what helps it grow, know what they would like to plant in it, etc. A person's garden is at the very core and it's important that that core be strong and healthy. If a garden is overcome with weeds, then I don't believe a person can ever possibly feel beautiful or proud of him or herself.

I will continue to keep a constant watch over my garden. I will continue to plant flowers, and I will continue to pluck out those pesky weeds that pop up every now and then. And perhaps, some weeds will never fully go away. That person really dug their seeds deep into my garden. That is also okay. No garden is perfect and my garden is certainly no exception to the rule. It gets better with every passing day, despite the ugly weather that sometimes rolls in. I see my garden flourishing over these next years, even through the stress of applying for colleges and everything else that occurs during a typical senior year. Most importantly, I will not let another person come into my life and destroy my garden. I am proud to say that my garden is strong now. Hopefully, it will only get stronger from here on out.

*****

Impossible = I'm Possible by Elizabeth Nunn

When I was little, I remember wondering what my future would be like when I was a grown up. From a young age I struggled in life, and I can't tell you my future without telling you my past.

I was born into a family with a mother who abused drugs and alcohol, and a father who suffered from depression and PTSD. My sister, who was only thirteen, took care of my little brother and me. By the age of four, the police came and took my brother and me away from our parents. We were sent to live with our grandparents. They told us that Mommy and Daddy had to work so we were going to stay with them for a while. A while turned into a year, and then that year turned into four years. By then I was eight years old, my brother and I had not seen our dad for two and a half years. The summer of 2006 he suddenly returned and life was the best it had ever been. We did everything together and then he disappeared again. That following January he was shot and killed, and we lost our dad forever.

Life went on and I made it into middle school, but I became very sad. By my freshman year I was very depressed and suicidal. The following summer I overdosed and was sent to the hospital for help. I came back, but then everything went to hell again. I was sent away from my friends and family for a year; while I was gone I had the best time and sometimes the worst. I was living in Indiana at a girls' boarding school that helped me a lot. I made some of the best friends I've ever had, but on June 30, 2015, I lost a very good friend to suicide and it changed me forever. I returned home that August and started a new life. I started going to a new school, and I had to make all new friends. Of course I was very nervous but also excited, because it's my senior year of high school. I'm enjoying my new school and people here are very nice--I have made great new friends who accept me. My teachers are very nice and really caring, and my grades are the highest they have ever been.

So now you know my past. I have accepted that my childhood was a struggle, but I will not let that consume me. It has been a blessing in disguise because it has given me the strength and drive to make my future the best it can be. I have the best fiancé and friend who has shown me that I can change the world. I love infants, children, and old people. From the time I was little, people always told me that I had a big heart for caring for others and from a young age I knew that my job in life was to grow up and become mother myself. I thought I would enjoy doing something where I would help people, so I thought I would like to become a nurse. I would get to do everything I wanted and I would get to work with the age groups I wanted, and make a difference in people's lives. However, when I found out that nurses have 12 hour shifts, I couldn't see myself enjoying that job. So I was lost and a little set back because I had not taken the SAT yet and people all around me were enrolling into colleges. I was stressed out but after all I had just come through, I wasn't going to let this get me down. I heard from a family friend that she attended York Tech and that she didn't take the SAT's either. She told me that all I would have to do is take their Compass test and I would be accepted. I started to look into what degrees that they offered and that's when I found out what I was going to be: a dental hygienist. I would only have to go to school for two years and I would immediately be placed into a job straight out of school, and my hours would be great for raising a family.

Now, I'm signed up for second semester classes at York Tech. I thought my family would be happy with me now. Well, my hopes fell on deaf ears. My parents love me very much but aren't satisfied with my choices for my life. But I still have so many more dreams for my future. I hope that after I finish school, my fiancé and I can get married and think about starting a family. I can't wait to move into my dream house and smile at my life, knowing that I have done well for myself.

I have shared my story with you to show that even though I have had a rough past, it has helped me to become the person I am today. So part of my goal for this essay is to speak to you--you who have suffered, you who are struggling. I want you to know that there is always someone who loves and cares for you, even though you may not see it. I, too, have struggled to understand that my parents truly want the best for me. So even though times right now may be hard and you feel like nothing is going right and that you would rather give up than fight on, promise me that you will fight on. I promise you that if you do, you will surprise yourself.

*****

Stepping into the Unknown by Timothy Sanders

I've always been told everything that I do now will reflect in my future. Now that I know that, I look back and think about all of the things I could have done differently. As a junior in high school, I think of all of the things that are soon to come. Knowing what you want to do after high school is very important because it not only reflects your career path, but also identifies you as a person. It shows intelligence and the skills that are required to master that job. When graduation comes around you experience many feelings, feelings that identify your thoughts towards college at the end of high school.

For example, worry may suggest that you may not know what to do next in life after high school. Many people are unsure of what to do after high school because there are many new choices to be experienced. You just have to be the one to make those choices.

When I was a freshman in high school, I always wanted to grow up so fast and to not be a kid anymore. Now looking back, I wish I could relive those moments. Now schools are trying to make us grow up too fast by making us take job surveys and shadowing careers that we are interested in. As I am getting closer to graduating, there are more jobs opening, thus making it harder to decide what I want to do. They give the students all of the ways to explore our options, but it's only making it more difficult for us to actually find something we like. Not only that, but when we find a career that we actually enjoy, we have to pick a college that we would like to go to. But when you find a college that you like, there is a chance that you won't even get accepted. Then again, it's not only schools that pressure us, it's also our parents.

Parents always say that they want the best for you, but sometimes the best is too much. About a year ago, I was having a conversation with my parents about my grades. I was taking three core classes, working and playing sports and I was struggling a bit with keeping up with everything. They kept telling me that everything that what I do now will reflect in the future. I knew that, but if i wanted to succeed and go to college I needed to do better. I then started to spend more time on my school work and by the end of the semester I had pulled up all of my grades. There is still a lot of pressure from them because a lot of my family didn't go to college and now I'm expected to not only go, but to get scholarships. What if my grades start to fall when I go to college? Everything will be new to me and maybe that will affect how I learn things. There will be new teachers, new students, bigger classes and a new environment. I think that that a new environment would be different, but I fear that I may not catch on as fast and I would have to try harder.

I envy kids in elementary school who already know what they want to do with their lives because I'm a senior and I still don't know. I'm interested in a lot of things, but it's hard narrowing it down into just one specific career choice. There are some things that I would enjoy doing more than others, but some don't pay as much. I've always been influenced to teach something to do with soccer. I have been playing it for a few years now and I feel like it's something that I would be interested in teaching. During the school year, I taught children's soccer on the weekends and I had a great time doing that, but I have recently experienced working at a new job. My friend's dad gave me a summer job doing electrical work. I enjoyed doing that but I don't know if I would enjoy doing that for the rest of my life. Our school had a representative from York Tech come to the school and talk about welding and electrical careers at the school. I talked to him about possibly going to school there and he gave me a card and told me if i am interested in one of those fields, he could help me get a job straight out of college.

I am still unsure of exactly what I want to do, but for now I have a better idea. I have enjoyed electrical work but if I decided to go into welding, my dad could probably help me. I still have a year to decide but I'm not going to rush things. I want for whatever I end up doing to be something that I enjoy. Soon it will be the end of high school and it will be time to grow up and take responsibility. It will be time for me to leave high school and time to make new memories. It will be time for me to make new goals for myself but most importantly, it will be time for me to take my next step in life and for me to finally make one of the biggest decisions of my life.

*****

Not All Who Wander Are Lost by Emilee Stohl

Every year, my family goes skiing for a weekend in Boone, North Carolina. We stay in a big cabin with a fireplace that heats the whole house, keeping everyone warm. My dad, my brother, and I spend the entire weekend on the slopes--my dad and I on the black diamond slopes, the hardest slopes, and my brother on the blue square slopes, which are also pretty difficult. My mom watches us from the viewing platform on the side of the ski lodge. She has always wanted to ski but is too afraid to try. When I was in seventh grade, our skiing trip took a turn for the worst when my dad became extremely sick and had to be rushed to the hospital. At first he had the flu, which turned into pneumonia, which turned into double pneumonia, which resulted in a life threatening condition known as ARDS, or Acute Respiratory Distress Syndrome.

Acute Respiratory Distress Syndrome is a condition in which fluid collects in the lungs' air sacs, depriving organs of oxygen; it is life-threatening. My mom stayed with my dad in the hospital every night for eight days, and my brother and I visited every day after school. One day the doctors talked privately to my mother and grandmother about making my father "comfortable;" in hospital terms, "comfortable" means making sure a person's last wishes are fulfilled and the family says their final goodbyes. Miraculously, my dad lived, and, although he has trouble with his lungs occasionally, he is fine now. There was another man in the hospital at the same time as my dad who also suffered from ARDS; he was 42 years old and unlike my dad, he died from this horrific disease. After this life-changing experience, my dad decided he wanted to see as much of the world as possible before it was too late.

Since that experience four years ago, we have been to Mexico, Iceland, the Bahamas, and almost every state in the United States; we have plans to go to Costa Rica this summer and an Alaskan cruise after this Christmas. Traveling is something I love to do, whether it is an overnight trip to Myrtle Beach or a ten day excursion in Guadalajara. Traveling is my way of connecting to the world; I get to experience different cultures and traditions first hand.

Going to Iceland this past November was a life-changing experience for me. When my mom first told me we were going to Iceland, I thought she was crazy! She wanted to miss my family's Thanksgiving celebration, with four different kinds of macaroni, a perfectly cooked turkey, a table full of desserts, and tea with the perfect amount of sugar, making it the sweetest of sweet teas, to go to Iceland. I complained for weeks about having to go to Iceland; I acted like we were going to be stranded on an island with no contact to the world, but that's not how it was at all.

We left on a Saturday and drove to Washington, D.C., where we stayed for the night, and on that Sunday, after watching the Carolina Panthers crush the Washington Redskins, we drove to the Washington Dulles International Airport to catch our flight. After waiting in the airport for hours, and eating our last meal in America, we boarded the flight and took off! Not only were the sights amazing, but the people in Iceland were, too. While waiting in the airport before our flight, I noticed this man, very tall, blonde hair of great length, and an awesome beard; as soon as I saw him sitting in the same area as us I knew he was from Iceland. I looked at my dad and pointed out the man with my eyes, we both agreed he was the stereotypical Icelander we had both imagined. We saw him later walking around the airport, and we decided to talk to him. The first thing I realized as we approached him was his shirt, with a big outline of Iceland and inside of that the words "born in Iceland" in large block letters. He told us all about what kinds of food to eat, what sights to see,

and he told us a little bit about his recent trip to Montreal where he partied a little too hard. He was the first Icelander we met on our trip and his friendliness gave us high expectations for the kind of people we would meet.
We landed in Iceland at around five in the morning, and, after waiting around for a while, our tour guide finally picked us up from the airport. We took the hour long bus ride to the city, Reykjavik, and our tour guide informed us that our hotel rooms wouldn't be ready for a couple of hours. At this point we had already been up for 24 hours straight, and we were all exhausted, so we did the most logical thing: go on a guided tour of the city. I was extremely tired and fell asleep about ten minutes into the bus ride to the first stop. After nearly two hours of sightseeing we finally made it back to the hotel, this time, however, our rooms were ready, and we were ready for our rooms! We quickly got our bags from the meeting room where they were being held, ran off to our rooms, and fell into the bed for the best nap EVER!

After waking up, we walked around the city some and enjoyed our first meal in Iceland. The food there was extremely different from our American food; they ate lamb dogs instead of hotdogs and they had a special seasoning salt they put on everything. I can't say I really enjoyed anything I had to eat while I was there, but I did have the best hot chocolate I have ever had from a small bakery called Sandholt; if you ever find yourself in Iceland, you should definitely try it! For the next few days we visited almost all the sights Iceland had to offer, from the Blue Lagoon to the Golden Circle. It was so amazing to me that, no matter where we were, there were always wild horses. My favorite day of the trip was the last day; before flying home, a man picked us up from our hotel in his large truck and took us to his farm, where his son was waiting to take us on a four-wheeler adventure. We put on the big snow suits they provided for us and then added on our own assortment of gloves, earmuffs, hats, scarves, and whatever else we could find to keep us warm. The ride lasted for a little under an hour, but during that time we rode through a river, up a mountain, around the top, and back down the mountain, and I also got to see some of the most majestic horses and glorious sights along the way. To my surprise, I was extremely sad to go back to the airport and fly back home.

I will never forget the places I saw or the people I met while in Iceland; the trip deepened my love for travel even more. I know my dad is pleased with his newfound travel experience and he will continue to cross countries off the map for many years to come. I wouldn't be surprised if my parents ended up moving to Iceland after retiring; they thought Iceland was the most wonderful place they had ever visited. Traveling has helped me understand different cultures and understand who I am as a person; I am a traveler. I cannot imagine my life without traveling; it has brought me so many experiences that I wouldn't trade for the world. I am usually a shy person but when I'm traveling I can be a totally different person who socializes with everyone; journeying helps me to open up and I find comfort in it. My absolute favorite place to be is in an airplane, high up in the sky, without a worry in the world.

I'm not sure which college I would like to attend, even though I have a small idea, but I do know that whichever college I choose, it must have a study abroad program. I haven't decided where or what I will study, maybe I could study environmental science somewhere tropical like Barbados, or maybe I could study culinary arts somewhere like France. I have even considered studying in Iceland because I loved it so much; it doesn't really matter to me where I go as long as I get to explore somewhere new, like I love to do. I have enough memories of adventures I've gone on while traveling to last a lifetime, and I wouldn't want it any other way. As the saying goes, "Not all who wander are lost." I am not lost when wandering; I am found.

*****

Beyond Labels by Jake Thomson

When I was five years old, I was diagnosed with ADHD and low spectrum Autism, and this was the moment my life changed. Simply because I was diagnosed with ADHD everyone looked at me differently, like I was strange. I was considered to be slow and I was treated ignorantly by teachers who didn't know exactly what autism was. Every week I was pulled out of class to learn basic social interaction. Unfortunately, they called me out of class publicly and told me to "go to Special Ed." Eventually other kids saw me as weird or stupid because I was always gone or alone, and this pattern didn't stop until sixth grade. However, I was never one to give up on myself. The labels society gave me pushed me to my limit and made me determined to prove everyone wrong. The natural ability most people are born with, how to read social situations, was the very thing I have had to teach myself. After all, it seemed no one else could teach me without humiliating me in the process.

There is one part of my past that I will always carry with me--it is what I consider my crucible and is the moment my life changed for a second time. In seventh grade, my parents felt that I needed to learn how to survive, and that would happen at Camden Military Academy. For the first time in my life I felt all alone, making choices about my academics and lifestyle. There was no social help or family to come home to, only myself. While I was there, I endured weekly beatings by upperclassmen until finally realizing that only I can stand up for myself, no one else. I will always remember David Cassie, the senior who taught me how to stand up. He was the only person there willing to help a seventh grader. David brought me to the gym every day after class, taking the time to help train me. Camden was my crucible and thanks to it, I know I can survive anything I face because I've gone through the worst.

Reflecting on my past is my secret to the future and is what fuels me each and every day. As I write this, it is easy for me to realize that the next step must be made from where my past has brought me today: a senior at York Preparatory Academy who's surrounded by friends and family; a member of several academic societies earned through my hard work and determination; the youngest leader at my church who is looked at daily for advice from those around me; manager and media producer for my youth group a daily commitment. I have responsibilities most people my age don't have because I work twice as hard. Ironically, the label that I was born with advises against leadership positions due to a lacking social compass or ability to read situations. And the very thing everyone said I can't do is the one thing I find my greatest skill and interests in: digital media. I have a passion for creating light sequences, for developing graphic and video editing, and especially for working around instruments with a soundboard tuning and adjusting them. This passion is one I constantly add to because my church teaches me more and more, helping me prepare for what I know my next step is going to be.

I have gone through my past and my current position how they have made me who I am today so I can finally move on to what the next step really is. Everyone my age has a similar next step: most of us will either go to college chasing after a dream or perhaps reinvent ourselves, while other might go straight into the working world to become who they always wanted to be. For me it's a little of both. I am choosing to go to Anderson University to learn all I can about digital media. My past has prepared me to walk into the next part of my life. It's exciting to realize that next year, unlike high school, I can focus on the passion and skills I have discovered like media or sound. I can dive right in learning and applying all I know with mentors who share this same passion. For some, a next step might be scary especially if you fear change or feel alone, but for me, it's exhilarating! One of my favorite things in my life are my friends and family; they are the reason I know my next step will be developing my passion with digital media. I can see myself using Adobe Creative Cloud working with Photoshop to help create presentations for businesses or using sound editing to help create a cd for my church's band. All this is great, but the next step for me is to create media and produce for Elevation Church because I want to be part of helping thousands of people by creating or inventing the atmosphere for them to worship--now that's my goal. And I can honestly say that it's truly within reach.

So now comes the time for us to part our different ways, whatever they may be. I only hope that you have pulled something from this or learned that hard work truly does yield results. When I was younger, I was ashamed or even embarrassed to talk about my past, especially the disorders. I was afraid that everyone would look at me different all over again but now I am proud to say that it's a part of me that makes me stronger. Thanks to this I know without a fact that no matter what the next step is, I can be confident in myself.

*****

Origin Story by Maiah Whitehead

Everyone has an origin story. Whether I hear a mild retelling of a person's childhood, or a more extreme account of their life's events, they will all tell you of how they overcame their barriers through hard work and perseverance. Determination can help you beat your past and clear the way for a bright, or for some, unclear, future.

First, let me tell you about one of my favorite superheroes: Spider-Man, AKA Peter Parker. Peter Parker is a smart, shy, and reserved teen, like myself, who gets picked on at school, but he has a secret. He fights crime and takes out the bad guys. As we know, he is one of the most well-known superheroes in the world! Parker battles enemies, such as the Green Goblin, Doctor Octopus, Mysterio, Kingpin, the Chameleon, and Doctor Doom, while I struggle with adversaries like asthma, social encounters, and this essay. Superheroes most definitely face intimidating foes, but I face different ones. The life of a superhero is, no doubt, a hard and dangerous one, things my life is not. However, the fact that, despite his temporary shortcomings, Spider-Man can seemingly surpass any obstacle is inspirational for me, and for many other young people, because we can identify with Spider-Man. He is just like me (although, admittedly, he is more cool and valiant).

I have asthma. Asthma is a lung disease that can range from mild to severe and essentially restricts your breathing. I, as a young child, had a more severe case. Asthma is an enemy that Spider-Man never had to face but I did and I found a way to overcome it. My asthma and annual hospital visits due to pneumonia--another one of my most intimidating opponents--kept me from school for long amounts of time. If I could beat asthma, a disease that I can never be fully rid of, I know I can face any problem that's thrown my way.

The rival introduced to me by asthma is discontinuity in schools. Private, public, charter, homeschool, Christian school...these are all included in my repertoire of school genres. I have experienced multiple curriculums, social environments, and educational tactics between these schools. Battles with sickness, convenience of curriculum, and a willingness to try out something new, led my mom to homeschool my older sister and me. At the time, my sister was in third grade and I was in kindergarten. My mom opted to teach both of us at the third grade level to conserve time. Homeschooling is one of the most immersive, hands-on approaches to education. My sister and I got to travel, be loud, and express ourselves to our hearts' content. Weekly trips to the grocery store served to teach us our math skills, as we calculated the price of items per ounce and added up totals. For our history lessons, we would drive to nearby historic sites and learn about our town's past. For science, we walked to the creek and found organisms to observe under the microscope. All this and more was featured in our wonderfully engaging education. I am immensely grateful that such an opportunity to learn in a hands-on environment with challenging material. I studied advanced math, science, social studies, grammar, and much more. That early learning helped to prepare me for the foes I now face: college prep, honors, and AP classes, making them exponentially less formidable. It also paved the way for college because conquering more advanced classes generally gives you a better chance of being accepted.

When homeschooling began to conflict with my parents' schedules, to my sister's and my own horror, we were sent to Christian school. This began the "Age of Oppression." Before I go on, let me inform you that the stifling component of this school was NOT the fact that it was Christian. Its repressive aura was the difficult part of the adjustment. We were forced to do immense quantities of work. We were subject to ruler slaps for disobedience. We were kept silent at lunch. Going from the degree of freedom I encountered with homeschooling to the strict nature of my first official school was daunting. It was, however, at this school that I learned to read and write, and the rigidity of the curriculum made my reading and writing skills develop efficiently. After Christian school turned out to be problematic, I went to private school. This transition was not as appalling, but it occurred right after the death of my beloved grandma, and these two events together made me less open and talkative. My grandma's death was like the death of Peter Parker's uncle: tragic. After a few years, it was time for another transition. My quietness had become overwhelming, so returning to homeschool was a welcome reprieve.

This time, however, it was different. It was, in the end, unsuccessful because of a lack of initiative, admittedly from me, and I once again, changed schools. After this switch, many more occurred, but they were not all negative experiences. In fact, I enjoyed the change. I was used to it. Switching schools so often helped me develop adaptability, a key skill for college readiness. School-related transitioning, as well as additional deaths in the family, aided with the continuation of my quiet demeanor. This has been one of my greatest opponents, an opponent Peter Parker has dealt with, and has kept me from reaching my full potential as a student. If I cannot overcome my shyness, how will I succeed when the days of college are upon me? Strong heroes can operate despite their disadvantages, so why shouldn't I? Spider-Man overcame it and he is just like me (again, he is definitely cooler).

Now to the present. As my life is right now, I am happy. I'm finally coming out of my shell, I'm enjoying my classes, working on my art... Junior year is my time to relax, and I intend to appreciate it to its full extent. AP classes may be hard, but I'm looking forward to more next year. Senior year will be filled with new AP classes, college applications, club meetings, and senior projects, and I know I'll enjoy these activities immensely. For now, I will continue to work hard, do my homework, spend time with my friends and family, and do what makes me happy.

For me, the future remains unclear. I suppose I could lie, and say that I want to be an astronaut, or an entrepreneur, or a superhero like Peter Parker, or some other amazing thing, but I see no sensible reason to. I have no problem in school and I consider myself to be an adequate, if not excellent, student. I'm respectful to my teachers, I get good grades, and these things supposedly set me above the norm and help me stand out to colleges who are looking for the best and brightest young minds, not just another average character. Nowadays, especially for adolescents like myself, college seems to be the central focus in most discussions. Where are you going to apply? What's your first choice? What about scholarships? These are questions my peers and I face. For those of us who haven't figured out all of the logistics yet, these questions are daunting and strenuous to answer. Some of us don't know the right answer. Hopefully, with the help of those around us, we can find the strength and courage to take the next step, a step away from where we are, a step towards being a hero, and a step into the unknown.

THE PLAN

College and Career by Tyler Billings

The next step for me is to finish out high school with good grades and take extra courses to get ahead in college. I would also like to do some college courses my senior year at York Tech to start earning college credits. I also plan to apply to college early in my senior year so I have a better chance of getting in. After I graduate high school, my plan is to go straight to college. I would love to go to Clemson University because that's where my mom and grandparents went and it is a very good school, but I think York Tech would be a better fit for me. I would still like to visit some local colleges just to see what else is out there but I'm pretty sure I will be attending York Tech. I don't really want to go to a 4 year college because I don't think I can handle college for a full 4 years but if I want to get a higher degree I would consider a it. Also I do not want to go to a college that is out of the state of South Carolina because I do not want to deal with traveling a lot back and forth. When I go to college I plan to major in Auto Mechanics. Auto Mechanics would be the best choice for me because I love to work on trucks, cars, and small engine things. This is the next step for me throughout the rest of my high school and college years.

I am currently a junior so I have one more year to go after this year, and I plan to make the rest of my junior year and my senior year be the best I have ever I had. For the rest of my junior year I plan to make good grades and get ahead in all of my classes. If I get ahead with all of my classes this year, my senior year should be easy and I can do York Tech dual enrollment to earn college credits. I have already been looking into colleges and what I want to major in and I think I have made a final decision but things can change in the matter of one year. Also, I plan to apply for college really early so I have a better chance of getting in. During my senior year I want to do the York Tech dual enrollment program that my school has, which will start giving me college credits and will give me a jump on college. If I don't do the dual enrollment program I still would like to go to York Tech, but I will most likely participate in the dual enrollment program because I want to get started on college so I don't struggle or have a hard time my first year. Those are my plans for the rest of my junior year and my senior year and what my goal is throughout both.

When I start college I want to major in auto mechanics because I have always loved working on cars, trucks and other small engine things and I would love a career field in that. I started working on small engine things when I got my four wheeler in first grade, and now I work on my truck. Auto Mechanics would be the best for me because I already know how to work on and fix some parts of cars or trucks and majoring in this field would build my knowledge a lot more. There are some things I definitely do not want to major in and that is a doctor or anything to do with teaching. My college plans are to attend York

Tech and major in Auto Mechanics. If I decide I do not want to do auto mechanics I would want to look into agriculture because I grew up all around farms and it would be cool to run my own farm, but auto mechanics is what's calling my name.

After college I plan to find a good paying job as a mechanic right away. I would like to start off working at a shop working for someone else, so I can see what goes on and how life is working in a shop. After working in a shop for someone else, I would love to open up my own shop and work on cars, trucks, and even small engine things such as ATVs and dirtbikes. I plan to make my shop a big name business and have a good reputation for doing good work. If my own business somehow doesn't work out, I will most likely just work for someone else in their shop. If I were to work in someone else's shop I would want it to be a family shop and not a worldwide shop. But if was last resort I might would work at a shop that is known worldwide and possibly stay and work my way up to the manager or the head mechanic. That's my plan for after college and what career I'm planning on pursuing.

Milton Berle said, "If opportunity doesn't knock, build a door," which can mean a lot of things. It can mean if you don't get offered a position or offered to a college you have to build the door to your future and do it all yourself. All my plans are set up to build my door to my future. My high school plan is to finish off with a bang and get a big jump on college. My college plans are to attend York Tech and major in Auto Mechanics. After college I plan to open up my own shop and if somehow that doesn't work out, I would want to just work for someone else in a shop or work in a shop that is known worldwide and work my way up to a high position such as the manager or head mechanic. The next step is not too far away but when it comes, I am ready.

*****

Fifteen Lessons by Peyton Chappell

Dear daughter,

I am currently seventeen years old and a junior in high school, and you're currently a fantasy I have in my head. Your name may be Vanessa, after your great-grandmother, or it could be Adelyn. You don't exist yet, but I think about you almost every day.

I have high hopes for you--not expectations, but hopes. I hope you live every second like it's your last one. I hope you cherish every friendship you have because one day those people may not be in your life anymore. I hope you never cry yourself to sleep at night over something a stupid boy did or said to you. I hope you have the courage to stand up for yourself and to never let someone walk all over you. I hope you have the trust in me to tell me every worry, fear, hope, and dream you have. I hope you are strong enough to know that you are perfect the way you are. Most importantly, I hope you put your happiness over everything else, including school and your friends. I hope you're the happiest young lady I've ever met.

Here are fifteen lessons I want you to learn in life.
1. **Some people will never like you; don't let it bother you.** I go to a school where I've been with the same people since I was in sixth grade, and some of them still don't like me. There are new people each year and not a lot of them like me. I don't let it bother me. Not everyone is going to appreciate your personality or cherish your laughter. It is not your job to make people like you.
2. **Don't pretend to be someone you're not to impress others.** Do not dye your hair blonde just to try and fit in. Do not lock your morals away deep inside your head just to follow the influence of others around you. Stick to who you are. Dye your hair pink and don't think twice about what someone will say. Stand up for the girl being made fun of because she doesn't know how to do her makeup. Be the spirited, kind-hearted young woman I have raised and know you can be.
3. **Get to know people personally instead of judging them.** Remember my example of the girl who's being made fun of for not knowing how to do her makeup? Well, I bet those other girls didn't know her mom isn't around to show her how to apply makeup. They most definitely don't know that she's not around because her mom lost her battle with cancer years ago. I am the girl that not many people get to know because I have a harsh exterior. I don't open up easily, I don't smile constantly; I'm not approachable. I wish for you to be different than me, I hope you make friends easily and smile often.
4. **Don't speed, especially on turns.** Also, please stop at stop signs.
5. **Not everyone deserves your trust.** You'll have friends who you will tell everything to, but then one day when the two of you get into an argument, she or he just might go off and tell somebody something you never wanted repeated. That friend didn't deserve your trust, they were not mature enough to handle your trust, but you still gave it to them. The cute boy who promises you the world and says they'll never leave you, does not deserve your trust. You are too young for a boy to make you promises like that. Do not believe everything a boy tells you; it will only lead to heartbreak. Your trust is a fragile thing, it's a part of your heart. You can only give it out and have it broken so many times before you're permanently broken.
6. **Put others before yourself, unless that person is an ex.** When your friends are happy, or when I'm happy, even when our dog is happy, you'll be happy. If you're anything like your grandmother or me, then you will be extremely good at this. No matter what, I want you to know you deserve happiness. Don't let an ex come between you and your new love. Do not worry about him; he will get over it. Don't let me come between you and what color you want to dye your hair. Make a list of things that make you happy. Make a list of things you do everyday. Compare the two and enhance your happiness.

7.   **Eat the dang pizza.** It won't kill you. Sure, it's greasy and full of carbs but you'll have time to worry about that later much, much later. Trust me you'll be a lot happier eating pizza than crying over a boy.

8.   **Your mom can see a fake friend before you can.** I had the hardest time learning this lesson. I never wanted to listen to your grandma; I always insisted she didn't know my friends like I did. She was always right. I've finally come to accept that if my mom doesn't think one of my friends is the friend she says she is then I need to take myself away from her. If I had listened to her earlier it would've saved me a lot of stress and hurt. What most people don't realize is that just like a boyfriend/girlfriend can break your heart so can a friend. If you put all this trust and time and effort into a friendship just to find out months later that that friend isn't giving you their all like you're giving them is crushing. And when the friendship is over and you see them having fun without you, it hurts. Choose your friends wisely.

9.   **Stop comparing yourself to others.** Everyone is different. Everyone has strengths and weaknesses, blessings and flaws. No one's hair falls exactly the way yours does. The lines in the palms of your hands are unique. Nobody else's eyes shine the way yours do. So what? You had a bad semester. You gained some weight. So what? You're single again. You lost your job. You'll try harder next time. No one is better than you because you're the only you there is; you're one of a kind.

10.   **Pray for your future husband.** He's out there somewhere, don't ever think he's not. I'm skeptical that I'll have a hard time finding your father but I'm sure he's out there. And I'm sure yours is out there too. You'll know when you find him. Pray for his wellbeing. Pray that he finds his way to you with as little heartbreak as possible. Pray that he makes smart decisions.

11.   **Don't let one mistake define you, but learn from your mistakes.** That D you made on your chemistry test doesn't mean you're dumb. It means you need to study harder, ask your teacher for help, and do better the next time around.

12.   **You were beautiful before he told you.** That boy, and yes that's what I will call him, did not make you beautiful. Your personality and heart makes you beautiful. The way you smile while playing with our dog. How you sing your heart out along with the radio while we're driving home every day. The way you laugh at my jokes. How you dance around the house like nobody's watching. Those are the things that make you beautiful. You are more beautiful than you will ever know.

13.   **Call your grandmother every day and always say I love you.** I know you don't want to have to answer a million questions or sit on the phone for what seems like forever. Just do it because you never think that the last time is the last time. You think there will be more, that you have forever, but you don't.

14.   **High school years are not the best years of your life, but enjoy it while it lasts.** You'll go into high school thinking it'll be the best thing ever--it won't. Sorry to burst your bubble, sweetie, but it's not like it is in movies. Other than the mean girls and the boys who don't really care--those are real,

63

very real. Watch out for them, but don't let them ruin your fun. Go to all of the home games, participate in spirit week, attend school dances whether you have a date or not. While you're in high school you'll think it's lame or nobody else is gonna go. Quit making excuses and go make memories because once you leave high school you'll regret not taking those chances.

15.   **You can't change people.** People are different you can't make someone be like you or want the same things you want. You can't force consistency, loyalty, or honesty. You can't force someone to keep their word, or communicate, or to realize something special is right in front of them. Things happen, life goes on. You focus on doing you and loving yourself and being happy, everything else will fall into place.

P.S. If I never have a daughter and you're a boy...I'm sorry, but I tried. Some of these will still apply to you. I love you.

*****

Overtime by Tracus Chisholm

It's the fourth quarter in the championship game with seven seconds remaining on the clock and we're down by two. The ball is in my hands and everyone is depending on me to make this last shot. I start to get nervous, but once the ball touches my hand, the adrenaline that rushes through my body knocks that nervousness right off. In the background I can heard the crowd counting down: "5, 4, 3…" while I'm rushing up the court, speeding past everyone. I finally get to the basket with one second left and I throw up a shot just as the buzzer goes off. Then out of nowhere everything just goes black. The next thing I know is I'm lying in a hospital bed and I start to panic, trying to figure out what's going on. The doctor finally came in the room and told me that I had a major concussion and I tore my ACL and my Achilles tendon. The only question going through my head at the time is, what about basketball? I was scared to ask because I didn't want to know what the answer was, but I had to know, so it just slips out. The doctor said, "Unfortunately, son, your basketball career is over." My eyes start to swell as tears run down my face, but really you can only ask yourself one thing… what's the next step?

I remember the first time a basketball touched my hands--it was like love at first sight. At a young age my mom always told me she could see I had a drive and determination that would make me successful in life. Since I was kid, I have been setting goals for myself that I'm still trying to achieve. Basketball has taken me places that I would never have thought of going and I can honestly say that little round ball has changed my life.

Throughout my life, I have spent countless hours in the gym and in the weight room. I remember waking up at 5 am every morning before school just to work on my craft. Most people see working out as hard and don't like doing it, but if you actually love the game you'd be ready to workout every day. I have a work ethic that most people don't have and I believe that is what separates me from other high school athletes.

Basketball has been there for me when nobody else has. When I was at my darkest, basketball brought me back to life. When I have a lot on my mind I can just go to the gym and all of those thoughts vacate. The gym is my holy place and where I can go to get away from everything. If anyone ever asked me what my utopia would look like, I would simply answer anywhere there is a court, a basket, and a ball to play with.

The game of basketball has brought about adversity numerous of times. At the age of thirteen, I went through one of the toughest times in my life. We were playing in a basketball tournament for travel basketball and as I was playing I kept feeling a very sharp pain in my left foot. I had to come out of the game because the pain was so bad. I eventually told my mother about the pain I was having and she just told me, "If it keeps bothering you, let me know." This is a day I will never forget: I was playing at the YMCA and I came down on my left foot. There was rush that went through my whole body and I was just lying there in excruciating pain. My mom came and picked me up from the YMCA and took me to the doctor's office. I went in there hoping and praying that it wasn't anything serious. The doctor couldn't tell by just looking at my foot, so they had to take me back for an x-ray. The doctor came back in the room and he told me I would never be able to play basketball again due to a stress fracture in my foot. My heart literally shattered and I think I cried for two days straight. The only thing I could do was to pray to the Man Upstairs and have a little faith. I had to go through physical therapy for a long six months; every night I had to do 100 calf raises which were very, very painful. I couldn't play the game I loved most for an entire year, which was extremely hard.

In my freshman year at Northwestern High School, I struggled at times. At one point I was failing two of my core classes and didn't realize it because I was so caught up in basketball. I learned quickly, though, because I had to sit out two games because I was on academic probation. I realized that academics is way more important than basketball because your knowledge will be there forever and basketball won't. It's hard being a student-athlete because you have to know how to maintain homework and school work with basketball. Once you learn how to balance your schedule, everything will become second nature.

I'm currently in the 11th grade and I attend York Preparatory Academy. I am on the varsity basketball and have set records for the school that might never be broken. After high school, I plan on pursuing my career as a student-athlete at the next level. I have a couple of offers from different schools, but I haven't decided which college I will attend. I want to take time and be patient with choosing my school because I want to make sure it's the best fit for me and my family. The decision will have a lot to do with the relationship the coach has with his players. To make sure I get there I have to stay focused, keep working hard in the classroom, and continue to work on my game outside of school.

As a kid I always wanted to start my business and open up my own boutique with rare sneakers and clothing. I recently changed my mind, and last year I decided that I wanted to be a personal trainer. I chose this field because it will keep me involved with the game I love most and with other young athletes who are trying to be successful in basketball. In order to do this I must go to college and major in kinesiology, the scientific study of human movement. With a degree in kinesiology, I can become a trainer at any level that I want-- middle school, high school, college, or professional.

As I look back on the past and all of the blood, sweat, and tears, I really have no choice but to wonder what does the future hold. My future depends on me and how hard I continue to work. I also know that the steering wheel is in God's hand and He's the only one who really knows what the future holds. I will continue to work hard both on and off the court and succeed in whatever He chooses is best for me. As of now, I believe He gave me a gift to play basketball and I will never take that for granted. Honestly, all that matters at the end of the day is to do what brings you joy in life, and basketball does that for me. The day that I stop having fun playing this game is the day I will hang up the jersey, and I don't see that happening for a long time.

*****

The Second Quarter of My Life by Khali Clegg

Throughout my high school career as a basketball player, I have prepared myself for my post-high school plans to continue to play the game that I love. From a young age I set very high goals and expectations that I plan to achieve. There are numerous things I wish to take action on, such as going to college and maintaining a set career path. Although my school of choice is unknown and my major is as well, I know for certain that I would like to participate in college basketball.

The game of basketball is an important part of me; it has been there for me when others were not. It has been a very consistent piece within my life. Basketball has been my refuge, a place where I have found my peace. Many bonds were formed with my teammates and coaches who assisted me through tough times, and I know they will be there when the tough aspects of my life decide to emerge again. Even though we will all separate eventually, my teammates are not just my teammates. They are my brothers, coach built this team to create a strong brotherhood and for us to play for one another. If you ever seen us play you could tell!

The relationship that I have built with the game has evolved over time. I have gained love, respect, and joy for the game in every single way. I have spent countless hours in the gym day in and day out to become great. I dedicated my time to the sport because I would hate to regret missing an opportunity. I want to live a content life, knowing that I gave it all each and every time. I treat every practice like I it may be my last. I never know when I may gain an injury or run into a serious obstacle that may be difficult to overcome.

When I was younger, my extended family went on a vacation, and some of my older cousins, aunts, and uncles were playing a pickup game of basketball. I had recently picked up the sport and became an enthused eight year old. I supposed I was pretty dang good! I had just been added onto my first official team at the YMCA, so I felt overly-qualified to play with my family. Unfortunately, my uncle predicted otherwise and stated that I needed a little more experience in order to "roll with the big dogs."

That experience has put fire under my feet, fire that has never been there before. I dreamed of "rolling with the big dogs." Rage filled my body instantly. In my heart I knew I was already a "big dog", an overly-qualified one at that I was big enough, smart enough, and good enough. I had to get better and I wanted to be the finest in the family. Better yet, I sought to become greater than anyone out there in the state. The expression my uncle used gave me the sudden urge to finally work to the best of my ability.

I am currently on the York Prep Academy basketball team. I play point guard which is also considered the "floor general." The duty of a point guard is perhaps the most specialized role of all positions. I am expected to control the team's offense by making sure the ball gets to the players at the right time. I figured by now since I've been maintaining that position since I started on the court I was well thought out to be a big dog.

Basketball has shown me much more than how fast I and strong I am. It has shown me that I am mentally tough and can work well through adversity. Certain situations that I have struggled with outside of basketball I've pulled through because I've struggled with something similar and connected them two together. Basketball showed me everything is not going to go my way, and also never give up easily on something because if it's worth having it shouldn't be easy.

College ball has always been a dream of mine and even though I may not have a definite school in mind, I have a couple offers to play. I am willing to join a team that will accept me as the athlete that I am. One aspect that I will be looking for when choosing my school happens to be the relationship the coaches have for their players, and how comfortable they make me feel being far from home.

I have chosen to extend my basketball career past high school for multiple reasons. One benefit that will most likely help me remain in school while enjoying the game is the fact that all schools offer tutoring sessions for athletes. Being an athlete is hard to balance. Your sport and school work in such a small amount of time longs for tutoring that would help me stay on top of my work. Another benefit I would be satisfied having is the connections the coaches may have to those interested in going to the pros. Lastly as an athlete, I will have the experience to take me to eventually coaching a big league team. If I were to run down such things knowing others may not have the same opportunities. I would call myself crazy!

There have been many nights where I planned out where I would go from here. There are also many nights where I have been too discouraged to continue. Either way I knew basketball was something I could never give up. My reasoning behind this is the fact that my love for the game defines me. Without it, it would be impossible to be the person I am today. Basketball is my stress reliever, entertainment, social aspect and my way out of Rock Hill. Saying that not to say I dislike the city I live in, I just know this isn't the right place for me and my family. I know there's more out there and I want to show my family that it's a better life outside of here.

So again you may ask, where I might be headed with basketball after this? Considering that there is a destiny for everyone and a plan for everything, I'll respond with, "Wherever God takes me." At the end of it all, He is the one that truly knows where I belong. So far, basketball has been His connection to me. If I am analyzing correctly, I would say that this is not going anywhere anytime soon. Basketball is my life.

*****

My Future by Brittany Crisp

As a high school student, I get asked about my future a lot. I've always had an idea what I've wanted to do in the future, but I don't have an actual plan. Well, the first step would be to finish high school. I'm almost done with that; I've got to take two more classes next semester and that's it. I'm excited to finish high school, but I might miss it after a while.

I need to keep my grades up and keep my GPA at a 3.5 at least. Mahatma Gandhi said, "The future depends on what we do in the present." So, in the present I need to be studying and making good grades, especially now that final exams are coming up. My mom told me if my GPA is a 3.5, my parents will help pay for me to go to York Tech, so I definitely want to take advantage of that offer. After I finish high school, the step after that would be to go to college. I've always wanted to go to college, and I always knew I would go. My parents have always encouraged me to go to college since I was little. I think it is necessary to go to college because I won't be able to get a job if I don't go. Ever since I was young, I've wanted to be a cosmetologist. Up until my junior year of high school, that's what I was planning to be. Cosmetology was something I was always interested in. I thought it'd be a good job for me. Because they say do what you love, right? This year, my junior year, things changed. I started thinking of other career options. I don't think cosmetologists make enough money. I know they say, "It's not about the money," and "Don't do a job just for the money," but in the real world money is important, especially once I move out and have my own family I have to support.

Another job I've always thought about having was being a dental hygienist. They make more money than cosmetologists. I looked it up online and it seemed like something I would like to do. So, I talked to my mom about it, and she thought it was a good idea. She said, if I wanted to, I could graduate my junior year and then, she said I could go take some classes at York Tech and go to school there. My cousin graduated early and went to York Tech and he seems to like it, so I'm sure I will, too. It sounds like a good idea to me so that's my plan for now. Graduate this year, go to York Tech, take all the classes I need to take, and become a dental hygienist.

Of course I want to take my mom up on her offer, because I'm ready to get out of here. I'm not implying that I had a bad high school experience. People say, "Your high school years will be some of the best years of your life," and I agree with that. I've had a pretty good high school experience so far. I've changed a lot, met a lot of new people, and tried a lot of new things. I think high school was fun, but I'm just ready to move on.

I hope I'm making the right decision, choosing to be a dental hygienist and not a cosmetologist. I could always go to beauty school later if I have any regrets. Also, I hope I'm making the right decision to graduate high school early, too. The guidance counselor tried to convince me to stay my senior year, and people tell me that senior year is supposed to be easy and really fun. Another option my mom suggested is to still go to YPA next year and I could just take some study halls and easy electives. I just don't see the point in staying when it's unnecessary. Why waste my time when I can be doing something productive in college? I don't want to go away to college. I used to want to, but, I don't think I could leave some of the people I have in my life behind. I plan to stay here and finish all of my schooling and then I'll think about moving. I kind of like it here in Rock Hill, but I think it'd also be fun to move somewhere different and have new experiences. It also depends on if I have someone to move with, because I wouldn't want to move by myself. I'd get bored. I'm not exactly sure what my future holds, but that's basically my plan for now.

*****

I Can't Wait by Jordan Faulkenberry

When I was a freshman, I could not wait to be a senior, I couldn't wait to go to prom, get out of school, go to senior week, and go off to college. I thought about the future all the time, but not really about the seriousness of it. I've had an idea of what I wanted to be and where I wanted to go to school since my sophomore year and I couldn't wait to graduate and go to college, but now that the time is here, it's a lot more scary and exciting than I ever expected. Your parents and teachers try to prepare you for the next step your whole life, and then suddenly that next step is now.

When I was little what I wanted to be changed on a daily basis. I wanted to be a hair stylist. I used to go with my Mawmaw some Fridays to the beauty shop when she would get her hair fixed, and that's why I wanted to be hair stylist. I also wanted to be a stay at home because I loved playing with my baby dolls and acting like a mom; I even wanted to be a doctor or a veterinarian. My older sister Hannah had a big influence on what I wanted to do--I thought she was the coolest person in the world. Everything she did I wanted to do, she was like my role model. When she graduated, she wanted to go to York Tech and become a nurse, so for the longest time that's what I thought I wanted to do. Then freshman year came and my best friend since kindergarten changed a lot. She started drinking, smoking, and partying, and I thought it was cool so I did, too. My big plans for myself I was going to go to a big party school somewhere near the beach and far away from my mom and dad. I was serious about school, but then my grades kind of went downhill and so did my attitude. I stopped wanting to be just like my sister. Then I stopped hanging out with my best friend as much because we both went to different schools. After I moved schools we stopped talking for the most part, I made new friends, and my grades improved. I made the final decision about my future during junior year.

The first semester of my junior year, Dr. Kennedy spoke to our class and he said, "Everything you do now will affect your future kids and family," and that's stuck with me ever since. Before he said that, when I thought about my future I only thought about myself. I wanted to go away from home. I really just wanted to go to college so I could get the "fun" college experience. I just wanted to drink, party, stay out late, and have a good time. I mean, that's what my friends and I have dreamed of since freshman year. Honestly, when he said that, it kind of scared me and it was definitely an eye opener because I hadn't ever thought about my life like that until then or my future family. I mean, I've always wanted to be a mom someday, but I never thought about all the decisions that I am making now affecting them. After he told us that, I thought about it for a while and honestly it helped me make the final decision about my next step. When I made the decision about what I wanted to be, I thought about my future kids and what job would have the best schedule so I could still balance family and my job. I want to give my kids the best life possible--if they play sports, I want to be able to be the crazy mom who embarrasses them for yelling too loud, just like my mom did for me. I want to be able to be there for all their school plays and school-related things. My parents have always been good at balancing work and family. They have never missed any of my games or anything school-related, but they still work enough to give us the best life they can. If I hadn't heard Dr. Kennedy's words, I would probably still be stuck deciding between a nurse and dental hygienist; although it scared me, it made me realize that your next step does not just affect you but other people you haven't thought about yet. Even though it is overwhelming and kind of scary to think about like that, it motivated me and made me realize the next step is worthwhile.

The next step for me is to pursue a career in dental hygiene. When I was younger I wanted to be a dentist, but then I realized how much schooling that was, so I decided that a dental hygienist was a better fit for me. I will be attending York Technical College because they have a great dental hygiene program. After completing the program I would like to get my dental hygiene license in South and North Carolina, so I will have more job opportunities. Dental hygienists have flexible schedules and that's one of my favorite aspects of the job.

I want to have a flexible schedule because after I am done with school, I want to settle down and get married. I hope when I get married that our relationship is like my mom and dad's. They have so much fun together and they still manage to love each other after being together for 26 years and after having four kids. I hope my husband is a hard worker and is as easygoing as my dad. I also hope he loves dogs just as much as I do. After I get married, I want to start a family. I want to be able to be there for my kids all the time, just like my mom and dad are for me. The flexible schedule will allow me to be able to spend more time with my husband and kids. When I was a kid, my family and I would go to the movies together a lot and I hope one day I can do that with my family, too. Most of all, I hope we are as close as my family is now. I want my kids to be able to talk to me about anything.

I have always wanted a house with a wrap-around porch and a white picket fence on a lot of land so my kids can have enough room to run and play in the yard like I did when I was little. My favorite memories include me being playing in the front yard with my sister. Whether it was running through the sprinkler, spraying the yard with the hose pipe just to make mud pies to throw at each other, or jumping on our trampoline; I'm really lucky to have those memories and I hope my kids will have them, too. If my kids accomplish what they want in life and my husband is happy, then at the end of the day my next step will have been worth it to me. After my kids grow up, I hope I'll get to be a grandma. I hope I'll be close to my grandkids like I am with my grandparents. I hope they beg to come to my house like I did to go to my grandparents. I hope I can sit on my front porch with my husband in our rocking chairs and be proud of what I accomplished by taking the next step.

*****

Creating a Better Future by Katelyn Forsythe

Abraham Lincoln once said, "The best way to predict your future is to create it." This quote is very powerful in saying that you can't just sit around and wait on your future to unfold, expecting that you will get somewhere great later on. You are in charge of your future and the choices you make today will make or break you in the end. I, for one, am going to do everything I can to create my own future.

I plan on graduating high school this year. It's hard to believe that we are all seniors this year. As I'm writing this, I look around the room and see faces of people I have known since elementary school and some new faces of the people I met only just this year. It's amazing to think in a few months our little class of sixty and some odd students we will be walking across the stage.

After I finish high school I am planning on going to York Technical College for two years to get my basic classes completed and to get a degree in business, so hopefully one day I will be able to open my very own restaurant. I love to cook! I have been cooking since I was about seven years old. I remember being in the kitchen with my grandparents helping out with our big family dinners, especially the time at thanksgiving when the sweet potato pie caught on fire in the oven. That sure was a dinner to remember. I like the idea of bringing people together to have a good laugh and to get some family time in around the table. You name it and I can make it. Anything from mac and cheese to a big roast dinner, I would like to stick to simpler "Home Style" cooking when it comes to the place I would like to run. It was my paw-paw Whitesides' dream to open his own restaurant; unfortunately, he passed away before he could do this. When I finally do open my little diner, I hope I will be making his dreams come true.

Not only will I be working on a business degree, but I also want a degree in radiology. Having a degree in business helps to pursue my dream for a restaurant, but having a degree in radiology helps to pursue a career that would be available if my restaurant didn't work out. If I attend college further than two years, then hopefully I will be able to go to the University of South Carolina or another one of these great colleges in the North and South Carolina area. I love the South because of the people and the idea of 'Southern Hospitality.'

I know that being a radiologist and owning a restaurant are two very different careers, but I have always had an interest in radiology ever since I got injured playing one of my favorite sports. I was in the middle of a pickup game of basketball with some friends at school. I went up for a hoop shot but when I came back down, I felt and heard something snap. A couple of my teammates heard the crack and asked what was wrong. It turns out I tore a few ligaments and tendons, and I now have a cyst inside my knee cap and a lipoma, which is basically a benign tumor on my upper shin, close to my knee. The pain was very extreme and since then I have had over fifteen x-rays and two MRI's. I've been through three rounds of physical therapy. If these problems still persist, I'll eventually have to have surgery.

If I hadn't messed up my knee so badly I'd probably still be playing and hoping for a scholarship. (Or should I say "hooping" for a scholarship?) Things happen for reasons though; plus, when have you ever heard of a basketball player who was only 5' 3 (other than Muggsy Bogues, of course) that got drafted into "the big leagues"? So I am kind of glad I am in this particular situation because it provoked an interest in a field of study that I wouldn't have given a second look too otherwise.

I would also like to minor in fine arts if I can. I know what you're saying: "This girl is crazy; she has way too many interests." But theatre and fine arts have always played huge roles in my life! I remember my first play: I was an angel in a church performance. I was about six years old and I remember being so excited about it. I didn't have any lines but my friends and I got to sing "Holy Night" it was my first taste of performing arts, and I've loved every bit of it since. I even know how to play a little bit of piano thanks to my Uncle Mike who taught me how to play a few verses of "Joy to the World" and I basically taught myself how to play the rest. My most recent performance was in a small skit at school. I was the mayor of a small town who had to solve a large crime that was committed. I may seem like the quiet type, but I love all types of visual and performing arts and I will take any part I can get! I also spend a lot of time drawing and have even entered a few competitions. I'm not the very best but it's what I like to do in my free time or just when I want to get things off my mind. Photography is also a big thing in my life. It feels like I am able to capture a moment in time and we will get to have a memory that will last forever. Whether or not the gig is big or small doesn't matter to me, arts have just always been a part of my life.

Out of all of the goals I have and dreams I've dreamt, I want to succeed most in making myself a good life and staying on track to create myself a promising future. I see myself living in Holden Beach, NC, working as a radiologist, starting up my own diner, dabbling in all the arts and playing a game of basketball with my family every once in a while. I give credit to all of the people who have tremendously helped me along the way. Among these people are my family, friends, teachers and coaches. I want to thank everyone who's helped me find my way to get where I am today. If it weren't for all of you, I don't know where I would be today.

*****

My New Chapter by Victoria Gaston

Wildlife Biology is the study of life's different ecosystems. Wildlife Biologists travel across the world and study the habitats, protect endangered animals, and record population numbers. They work with animals both on land and in water. They must be ready to deal with ecological, social, and political problems dealing with endangered species. Wildlife Biologists are employed primarily by state and federal agencies, but there are other areas of employment.

Wildlife biology has only been the most recent career I want to pursue. In elementary school, I wanted to be a veterinarian, but at the end of middle school I didn't know what I wanted to be. I had millions of new ideas swirling around my head of things I could do. Astronomy, teaching, marine biology, artist, a baker, even a horse trainer and riding instructor. At times all those seemed fun and exciting, but then I would either forget about them or decide that it wasn't for me.

Now in high school, I was able to narrow it down to two career bases-- teaching and biology. I knew that if I went into teaching, kindergarten would be where I would go because of my past experience working with them in the after-school program here at YPA for three years, but in biology, I didn't know what I was going to do. My parents tried helping me, giving me pros and cons of both careers and sending me emails and texts about the vast fields in biology from websites they found; my Papaw would look up colleges with programs in biology and teaching, my cousin Emily and I would talk about careers and colleges together, but it was the person I least expected that somehow helped me discover wildlife biology.

Five years ago a new member joined my family. Her name is Lily, she is the youngest of my family, and is the most hyper person I have ever met! She loves messing with me and my brother (he swears she is trying to kill him sometimes), and every time we see her, she always wants to be with us. One of her favorite pastimes, when we have to be quiet and not run around, is watching her favorite shows on Netflix. One night at her house, while trying to get her to calm down and go to sleep, I turn on her favorite show, *Wild Kratts*. I still don't know what was different about that night, but for some reason I was really intrigued. I knew that the hosts, brothers Martin and Chris Kratt, had another job besides being the hosts, and I decided to look up what it was. That's when I somehow discovered Wildlife Biology as well as Zoology. I started researching what they were and the difference between them. I learned that Zoology is a branch of biology that relates to the animal kingdom and includes the structure, embryology, evolution, classification, habits, and distribution of all animals both living and extinct as well as how they interact with their ecosystems, whereas Wildlife Biology is the study of life's different ecosystems, and biologists in this field study the habitats, keep population records, and help preserve endangered species. Zoology is the branch, and Wildlife Biology is a field within that branch.

Before, I was trying to decide my future with my head, listening to pros and cons and trying to see what everyone's reaction is with both careers and trying to please them and make them happy with what I choose, but a few months ago I decided to take a different approach. The school took a field trip to Winthrop for the college fair and I knew I had to decide on a career soon. On the bus ride over I started thinking with my heart and decided to think about what would make me, and not everyone in my family, happy. When thinking about teaching, my heart had a sort of hole in it. I knew I could be happy with it, but I didn't know for how long. When I started thinking about biology I felt somehow free. I don't know how to describe it in words that will fully express how I felt, and how I still feel, besides using all the synonyms for cheerful, happy, excited, ecstatic, proud...like I had finally found my place in the world. It felt as if a new door had opened up, like a chapter in my story had finally ended and a new one was just beginning to be written.

*****

Jumping into the Unknown by Jonathan Grant

I hope to go skydiving over the summer before I head off to college. The idea of skydiving sounded scary at first, but I decided that this is something I've always wanted to try and it's something I've set my mind on doing. It's like what Wayne Gretzky said: "You miss one hundred percent of the shots you don't take." I think this quote is important because it is not only applied to hockey but can be applied to almost everything in life. I think we should all do what we love in life and we shouldn't settle for less. Honestly, if you are capable of being the best at what you do, why not pursue what you love? Life will throw things at you but you have to learn to dodge them. Some people may say this seems like a bucket list, but it's something I want to do before college because after college, you have to make rational choices. When life gives you lemons you make lemonade, and when life gives you opportunities to do what you want in life, you take those opportunities. What I love most about college is that I will be on my own for the first time and it's up to me to do the work necessary to graduate.

Most jobs require a college degree; in fact, around 60% of the jobs globally require a degree after high school. So in order to be in that 60% I need a college degree. Without a college degree you would be competing with people for the other 40% of jobs and most of those jobs' salaries are a lot less than most jobs with a college degree. One thing I know for sure is I will go to college. I've put too much effort into school to not go. School is something I've always dreaded, but I think of college as something to look forward to because if you don't do the work it's on you--there is no one to blame but yourself. It's a sign of freedom and responsibility and it's something I know that I can use to prove to myself and my parents that I am a responsible young adult. I know for sure that I don't want to be flipping burgers at McDonald's. I'm not saying there is anything wrong with that, but if you are capable of more, then why settle for less? I want to be happy throughout the day not just at the end of the month when I receive my paycheck, and not be upset with my job for the rest of my life. I don't want to be stuck in a career where I will wake up every morning and hate what I do; I want my job to be something I thoroughly enjoy.

My next step after high school will be to go to a four year college and get a bachelor's degree in marketing. I hope to use this marketing degree to help companies market their products or services efficiently and I want to go to college so I can make myself more marketable. As for which college I will go to I have not decided, but I have narrowed it down to the last two, College A and College B. I've already received my acceptance letters from both of these schools. At College A, I would be 10 minutes from my house and I would be able to be a commuter and not have to stay on campus which would lower the price by a lot; however, I feel that it may limit my college experience. College B might be the college for me since I am the kind of person who doesn't like to get out of their comfort zone, but college B is three and a half hours away from my house. Also I'm a rather quiet person and if I were to go there I would be forced to get out of my comfort zone which is something I believe is necessary for college and in life.

Your future is a lot to think about, but even in high school you have time; just make sure to not wait till the last minute. I believe that we all have greater potential than we believe--we just need to strive for it. I don't want to look back in life and realize that I never fulfilled any of my dreams. In life, dreams are the keys to happiness. I know that I need to pursue these dreams in order to make something of myself. I know that some people get angry with themselves because they are afraid of what they have become, they don't like their jobs or they just aren't happy in life and I won't just sit around and let that happen to myself. I will jump out of the plane if need be and even if I stumble, I will land on my feet and continue to move forward.

*****

Taking the Shot by Monta Houston

It's the last game in the NBA Finals between my team, the Charlotte Hornets, and the Golden State Warriors. We are down two points and there's ten seconds left in the game. I, the star player for the Charlotte Hornets was having a great game so far. I had scored a career high of fifty points. My teammate takes the ball out of bounds and passes it to me. I dribble down the court and shake a few defenders. There's two seconds left. I shoot the ball. Cameras are flashing and everyone's eyes are larger than usual. The ball goes through the net just as the horn sounds and everyone jumps up and cheers. We have just won the NBA Finals! As I was running and celebrating, I kept hearing this distant voice in my head. For some reason, it was yelling, "Wake up." but I continued to celebrate. After one final "Wake up" that was louder than the rest, I opened my eyes and sat up in my bed. It turns out that I was just dreaming.

Just think about these two questions for a few seconds. What if you could have the job or career that you've wanted ever since you were a little kid? What if you could just wish for your dream job and it would come true? Of course, neither of these things are possible, that's why they are "What if .." questions.
Ever since I was a little boy, I always wanted to be professional basketball player in the NBA. To this day, that is still my dream. Growing up, adults would always ask me what I wanted to be when I grow up. I would always tell them I wanted to be a professional basketball player. Then they would proceed to ask me what my backup plan was. I never quite understood why they would ask this question. "If I already knew what I wanted to be, what's the point of thinking about another career?" I would think to myself.

As I grew older, I started to realize that not many people were able to play professional basketball. There just aren't enough spots on a professional basketball team. Also many athletes get career-ending injuries in high school and college. As I got to high school, the new questions on the table were, "What if I don't make it to the NBA?" and "What if I get an academic scholarship and not an athletic scholarship?" I never even took the time to sit down and think about these questions until I got to high school. In middle school, I began to realize that I really enjoyed drawing and that I was good at it. So when I got to high school, I started exploring careers that involved drawing and designing. After talking it over with my parents, we decided that my backup career is graphic design.

Every day I hear people say that no one makes it out of Rock Hill for basketball. Hearing this just motivates me more to work harder each and every day. On a daily basis, I've started lifting weights before practice, practicing on my jump shot, and working on my ball handling. I even watch videos of professional players so I can study the way they play and figure out what I can do to improve my skillset. I play basketball for our school team and we usually have practice Monday through Thursday and Sunday unless we have a game on any of those days. After practice, I go to the YMCA and put up more shots. I'm very dedicated and no one can tell me that I can't make it out of Rock Hill for basketball. I feel like the sky's the limit for me, and it is.

Playing varsity basketball for York Prep has been one of the best experiences of my life. I am closer with my teammates this year than any other teammates I've ever had. We have bonfires and sit around the fire and tell stories and tell each other why we play basketball. Now when we play, we play for each other. We can call each other at any time and we can rely on each other for anything. They aren't just my teammates though. They are my friends, my brothers. We have a great coaching staff as well. I've learned a lot from our coaches this year. I know I can ask any of them if I need help with anything and I appreciate everything they've done for me. The team is like one big, second family to me. At the end of the day we all love each other.

Not only do I play for my school, I also play travel basketball over the summer. The position I play is point guard. The point guard is in charge of controlling the team and getting his/her teammates involved. My favorite basketball player to ever play is Allen Iverson--he always gave 110% effort and I can relate my game to his because he was one of the smallest players on the court. Growing up while playing basketball, and even now, I am always one of the smallest players on the court. At times it was really difficult for me going up against bigger players. But as my game has matured, I've learned to play smarter than everyone else on the court. I've learned that I actually have an advantage over bigger players; I can use my speed and quickness to easily move past them. I have very good decision-making skills and a very good IQ for basketball. As a result of this, I led the state of South Carolina in assists, with seven per game.

Balancing academics and basketball is not an easy thing to do, especially since I'm in honors classes. Having basketball practice at night has led to many late night homework sessions. I truly love basketball, but I never forget that my education is more important. There have been lots of times my mom has asked me," If you get a basketball scholarship offer to a small school or an academic scholarship to a larger school, which one would you choose?" Every time she asks, I choose the academic scholarship. When I start applying to schools, I want to make sure that they have a good arts/graphic design program before I look into the basketball program. I'm interested in a few different schools for the next step of my life, which include: Coastal Carolina University, Clemson University, Charleston Southern University, College of Charleston, Presbyterian College, and Anderson University.

I want to play basketball in college for a few different reasons. One reason is because I'd get to continue to play the game I love. Another reason is because it's a chance for me to help pay for my college tuition. My last reason is because I know it would make my parents proud, and I love seeing them smile. What does basketball mean to me? Well, let me just tell you. Basketball is the love of my life. It's not just a sport, it's my passion. It's my escape from the rest of the world. When I step on the court, I zone everything out. I give it my all every single time. Basketball has also helped me grow as a person. There have been times when people have doubted me. There have been times when I doubted myself, but when I stepped on the court, all the doubting disappeared from my mind. I used to get down on myself a lot when I messed up. I just had to remember that everyone makes mistakes. Mistakes are just a part of life. I have worked on remembering that I just need to go out there and have fun. Without basketball, I wouldn't be who I am today. It has helped me learn who I am. I've made many friends while playing basketball as well. The memories that I have with basketball will be with me forever.

I will never give up on my dreams
because my love for the game is more than it seems.
I'm just a small town kid with worldwide dreams,
who shows no mercy for the other teams.

I always tell myself, "Life is a canvas and it's up to you what you paint on it." I know I could never paint a perfect picture but I want to paint the best picture I can. So what is my next step? Who knows? Whatever my next step is, just know I'm going forward.

*****

"Make Many Plans" by Maddy Knox
"You can make many plans, but the Lord's purpose will prevail." Proverbs 19:21

Twelve years of school and I never knew what I wanted to do when I graduate. I didn't know what school I wanted to go to, what I wanted to be, or what my interests were. I've had many classes and teachers all trying to help me find out what I wanted to do in my life. Some made me think long and hard about some choices. I've had many jobs and schools that I have seen and heard about catch my eye. I've prayed that God would show me where my life should go and where I needed to go from where I am now. I chose this verse because it really just connects with what God says about His future for us.

"You can make many plans..." I've set my mind on so many schools and jobs that I would actually be willing to do in my life.

Some for example are Welch College in Nashville, TN; Pensacola Christian College in Pensacola, FL; Horry Georgetown Tech College in Conway, SC; Coastal Carolina College also in Conway, SC; Spartanburg Methodist College in Spartanburg, SC; and Spartanburg Community College in Spartanburg, SC.
Among all the school choices I've considered many job titles for myself, like marine biologist. I love everything that has to do with the beach and I would love to learn more. I could help out everything in the ocean and learn more about it. I could be a Registered Nurse (RN), because I've always wanted to be in the medical field and I feel like I would be very good at taking care of other people. I've also thought I could be a Medical Assistant, because my papa, who I admired, was a doctor and I would love to try to strive to be like him in some ways. I could be a therapist because I am a good talker and listener and I always try to help people if I see them sad or I think they are going through something I try to make them feel better and I like hearing other people's problems. I've always wanted to be in the service, so I have thought about being a military nurse, but I don't think I could handle killing other people so why not take of the people who protect us and once again its medical and I

would get a lot of benefits and I could travel. I might be a surgical tech or phlebotomist because its medical and I think it would be a cool job. Cosmetology and styling hair is something I've always pretended that I was going to do. I would still love to do it because there's a girl thing about doing hair, and I've always thought of myself as a girly-girl. It's the job that I always wanted as a little girl and had a passion for. As you can see I've had problems with seeing what I want my life to be like and what I want to do.

In my life I will have to make many plans. I personally believe that after the many years of looking through job titles and schools that I really know where I want to go from here. My plans when I graduate is to become a Phlebotomist and attend Spartanburg Community College. I believe that it's a right fit for me, because they have more than 100 programs to pick from, it has the lowest tuition in the upstate, it also has strong student support service. I will attend there in the fall of 2016. Many events will happen with my life before I get there, but I will not worry because God will show me what I should do.

"...but the Lord's purpose will prevail." I believe so much in my quote because He will help you when you ask.

My faith is important to me because of the many times in my life where I was alone and didn't really know what I wanted for myself and my life. My faith has given me so much hope to just keep holding on and working on bettering myself. My faith in God has helped me become who I am and where I am at in this point of my life. My faith has showed me that I do have hope in this world. As a Christian I have a purpose: to live my life for God. What I do in this world reflects on Him, with His help and guidance. That's the importance of my faith.

I hope that five years from now I am working and making money and maybe have a family after I graduate my college classes. I also hope to have a house and maybe pets as part of my new family. Things in my past have made me the person I am today. I can be like most people and say that I've been through so much, but I know now that I need my life to be together and in order. In my life I want to be have no worries when it comes to food and clothes, I want to have everything I need; I have faith that following God's path will provide me with what I need to be happy and healthy.

*****

My Pinterest Bucket List by Aubrie Midkiff

I started using Pinterest when I was in seventh grade. I love Pinterest because I can see ideas I have never thought of and can keep up with the latest fashion trends. Another reason I absolutely love Pinterest is it can help plan my dream future without actually having to spend money; I have already planned my

wedding and I'm not even close to getting engaged. Most of the people I follow on Pinterest have some form of a "Bucket List" board. So here are some the things on my Pinterest bucket list:
1. Travel the World -- Before I die, I want to be able to say I got the opportunity of a lifetime: the opportunity to travel the world. I want to see London, England; Sydney, Australia; Rio de Janeiro, Brazil; and Mumbai, India. I want to go to London, England, because the British people have amazing accents and also I want to experience what life would be like in another country. When I start traveling I want to start with England because the language barrier is hardly there unlike Brazil, where the people speak Portuguese. Sometimes I can barely speak English, let alone a language that is completely foreign to me. I want to visit Australia because I want to see kangaroos and koala bears in their natural habitats. Koalas are super cute and I really want to see a koala bear cub in my lifetime. I want to visit Rio, because I want to see places that the Olympics will be held. I actually want to go see the Olympics in person, but I don't have the money right now, so when I get older that is another thing I want to do. I want to visit India because in my World Religion class we saw a video about Holi, which is also known as the festival of colors. The festival celebrates the victory of good over evil. I want to be a part of the festival because it lets me know that there is still good in the world even with all the hate that is also in it, and that good will win over evil.
2. Let Go of Floating Lanterns in Thailand -- My favorite Disney princess movie is *Tangled*. *Tangled* is my favorite Disney movie because Rapunzel has really long hair and when she became my favorite princess, I had really long hair, too. And Flynn Rider is undoubtedly the most attractive Disney prince, and they get married. I really want to be able to see all the lanterns in the sky like Rapunzel did. Also I want to go see the floating lanterns is because of what the lanterns symbolize. The lanterns symbolize all your worries and problems floating away, which I think is pretty dandy. I don't like talking about my problems, so letting go of lanterns would be a way to let go of my problems without actually having to talk about them.
3. Be A Role Model -- I want to make an impact on someone's life and be someone who young people look up to. My first role model was my mom, because she was a stay at home mom for a large part of my childhood. My mom was my Superman with three kids, trying to balance everyone's schedule and trying to get everyone where they needed to be when they needed to be there. Sure, sometimes we were late, but she did the best she could, and for that, I look up to her. In fourth grade I went to my first public school ever, because I was homeschooled before. My mom also went back to school to become a Dental Hygienist. Seeing her study and try to get everything done made me want to work hard in school, so I aspire to be like her and

get good grades. Just seeing my mom try so hard to do everything made her a good role model for me. Another role model that I have is Audrey Hepburn. She is a wonderful role model because she was a humanitarian; she volunteered in Africa, and Asia. Volunteer work is important to me because the work you do truly helps the community around you, and that eventually helps the world. Having strong role models makes me want to be able to be a good and dependable role model for young kids. Even if I am only one person's role model, I know I have changed someone's life.

4. Donate Blood -- Since 9th grade, I have wanted to donate blood. I want to able to say that I have saved a person's life. I tried to donate when I turned 16, but since I'm scared of needles my blood pressure was too high and I couldn't do it. I have had to have my blood taken in those tiny little vials and I still pass out. When I was eight, I had to have my blood taken for the first time, and I remember that my mom wasn't allowed to go back with me and so I was already freaking out. Then the nurse pulled out the needle and I started crying because I was so scared. When it was time to actually take the blood, she said, "You have small veins so this gonna hurt even more than normal," which is not something a nurse should tell an 8 year old. When the nurse finally put the needle in my arm, my veins rolled, and guess what she did? She just dug around in my arm until she found the vein. I started to scream and cry even more, and she just continued taking blood. So now I'm terrified of needles and getting blood taken, but I want to overcome my fears to help save a life.

5. Pay a Stranger's Bill at a Restaurant -- One time my mom and I were at a drive-thru and my mom was about to pay the worker for our food, and the worker said that the person in front of us had already paid it. My mom and I were surprised but said okay. My mom then saw a car behind us and decided to pay for their food. I guess some people wouldn't give this a second thought but I thought, "What if this happened in a restaurant? Would it continue throughout the restaurant or would it stop on somebody?" Seeing the movie *Pay it Forward* in Pre-Calculus made me really want to continue the small acts of kindness that have happened to me.

6. Grow My Hair to Donate for Cancer Patients -- When I was younger, I saw my sister donate her hair to Locks-Of-Love, which I also wanted to do, but my hair wasn't long enough. In fifth grade I decided to let my bleached hair grow super long so I could donate it, but I didn't read the requirements for donating, which prohibit bleached hair. Then I cut off the bleached part of my hair, started to grow it out again. In 8th grade my hair was finally long enough again, I read the rules for donating again to double check and I thought I was good to go. The problem this time was my hair wasn't exactly the "healthiest" and the Locks-Of-Love people want healthy hair for the wigs, so I just got a regular haircut. To this day I am still trying to

grow my hair long AND healthy, so that when I graduate I can donate my hair to a cancer patient or someone else in need.
7. Buy My Dream Car -- My dream car is a Range Rover Sport Supercharged Dynamic. I think that it is a beautiful car and I know it will be hard work that allows me to achieve this dream. I plan to reach this goal by going to college and becoming a Chemical Engineer. I want to become a Chemical Engineer because I love chemistry and think it would be cool to see how it applies in everyday life. I know that I won't get my dream car right away or probably even five years after college, but knowing that I want it gives me a reason to work hard and to never give up.
8. Live On My Own -- I want to live by myself so I can learn how to be truly independent. I want the responsibility and the consequences of my actions. Along with living by myself, I also want to adopt a puppy, so that way I can prove to myself that I can take care of another living thing. I want to be able to use my "Dream House" board on Pinterest and design my own house. I'm excited to eat whatever, whenever, especially Chinese food, which I love A LOT!

These are just a few pins from my "Bucket List" board on Pinterest. I plan to start my bucket list as soon as I graduate high school, but realistically I won't start until after college. All the things on my bucket list are important to me in some way, it might be as little as going on a road trip with my friends, or as big as add a lock to the Love Lock Bridge in Paris, France, or stay in Cinderella's castle at Disney. My bucket list is more of a list things that I want to achieve rather than a bucket list, so I guess it could be called an achievement list. My list represents me and the things I want to accomplish and now I have a plan on how to obtain them.

*****

Resilience, Patience, Loving Guidance by Mallory Pannell

Sugar, spice, and everything nice, that's what little girls are made of. Snips, snails, and puppy dog tails, that's what little boys are made of. So what are teachers made of? Resilience, patience, and loving guidance--that's what teachers are made of.

So, now that I have decided what I want to do with my life, everyone will ask different kinds of questions. When will I get married? Have I thought about starting a family? What am I looking for in a future spouse? Blah, blah, blah. Questions like these I can't answer. Unlike the questions about picking a college, major, or career, these questions are not just about me and what I want. Would I like to get married? Someday, yeah. Do I want kids? Without a doubt. But these are decisions that take a team effort to decide. So if I can't decide these things all on my own, why would people constantly pester me with such senseless questions?

As soon as I became a high schooler, I was plagued with the decision of picking a major. What if my dreams didn't require a specific major? Since elementary school, I have possessed a love of reading. And that is probably why, for a while, I was more than sure that I was destined to own a bookstore. At some point, someone so kindly pointed out to me that people are slowly forgetting about actual paper books and opting for electronic ones. I would likely starve if I opened a cute little bookstore, so I began to look for a new dream.

In middle school I took up sewing, this I just knew would be my life's work. My mom signed me up for sewing classes through 4-H and sewing quickly became my new passion. Under the instructor's gaze, I could sew with ease; however, sewing at home was a different story. Without Mrs. Barbara around, I found myself thoughtlessly making small mistakes, which almost always resulted in me crying and throwing my failed sewing project on the floor. Sewing was clearly not my niche.

Then, I got the idea stuck in my head that I was meant to be a teacher. Sadly, my dreams now meant college was a must.

So obviously, my next step in life is college. I know how people work when talking to high school kids, so let me save you the trouble of asking: no, I do not know where I want to go to college.

While I do not know where I want to go, I do have an idea of what I want to do with my life.

As soon as I graduate college, you can find me in a classroom. While I would much prefer teaching kindergarten to third grade (kindergarten and special education being the top choices), any elementary school classroom would suit me just fine. Yes, I know it will be hard. Yes, I know sometimes I will see or hear things that will break my heart. Yes, I know there will be more paperwork than I could have ever imagined. But if you think that I can't do it, well, that's where you couldn't be more wrong.

Unlike some girls who enjoy putting all of their focus on planning a wedding, I would much rather imagine myself decorating my first classroom...On the first day I walk into a bleak room. Plain walls, plain floors, plain desks. After taking in the space--after considering all the possibilities--I go straight to my desk, desperate to find some colorful decoration ideas on Pinterest. In one week, the students will return to school and I am certain that the currently austere classroom will dampen their high, five year old spirits. The door must be decorated first; after all, it's the very first part of the room they will see. I settle on modeling my door after one on Pinterest that was inspired by the Pixar movie, Up. The door will be covered in black paper, with a colorful house centered on the bottom of the door. Attached to the rainbow house's chimney are the strings of a bouquet of balloons in every color imaginable. Each balloon will be decorated with a student's name and birthday. Above the door reads, "Where Our Adventures Begin." Satisfied with how the door turned out, I relocate my crafting tools and start on the classroom itself.

An envelope falls off the kitchen table, bringing me back into my current reality.

I sit at the kitchen table surrounded by college acceptance letters. One week left until I have to make a decision. I slowly eliminate universities one at a time. After sitting at the table for hours, I have narrowed it down to four colleges. I decide that's enough hard work for one day and abandon the letters for a good book instead.

*****

Making Life Beautiful by Brandi Patterson

Soren Kierkegaard said, "Life is not a problem to be solved but a reality to be experienced." High school is tough, but it's something that we all have to go through. No matter how hard things might get through school, there's always help for you and you shouldn't have to struggle. High school is supposed to be about making friends, having fun, and finding a career choice. For many of us seniors our future is right around the corner and time's almost up. Personally I think the world outside of high school sounds scary and overwhelming, but we all have to face it sooner or later.

"What do you want to be when you grow up?" I can't tell you how many times I have been asked that question. I used to say things like doctor and lawyer. Then, of course, reality hit when I got to high school and I actually figured out what a doctor did and what kind of schooling a lawyer had to go through. My mindset, my friends, my personality, and my career choice changed a lot after my sophomore year. For a lot of people high school is just about passing and making it to the next year. I didn't start taking high school seriously until my junior year because it finally hit me that I only had two years left. School has never really been my favorite place. I would dread having to wake up early and go sit in a classroom for eight hours a day learning. I would come up with every excuse in the book to be able to stay home or to go in late. Most of the time it didn't work, but sometimes I could get away with it.

It wasn't until a few months into my senior year that I knew what I wanted to do after high school. I have always had a thing for doing hair and makeup. I love to watch people get their hair or makeup done, and I especially love the reaction they get when they see the final results. I enjoy seeing their eyes light up and the smiles on their faces. I want to be able to make people feel beautiful or handsome and be happy to go out and be confident about how they look. I know a lot of people say girls shouldn't wear makeup because it's "false advertising," but if that is going to boost someone's confidence and make them feel good about themselves then let them do what they want to do. I don't think that you should be limited to how you want to look I don't think society should have a say in how you do your hair or your makeup. So many people are quick to judge a person just because they don't like the way they look, which is a lesson I have learned myself.

My biggest supporter would definitely have to be my mom, who has always been there for me in any big decision that I've had to make. My mom has always been very supportive in everything that I've wanted to do career wise, and she really helped me in making a decision in what I wanted to do after high school. My mom started selling makeup when I was about twelve, so I was introduced to it at a very young age. She has taken me to three different schools in South Carolina to tour so I could make the best decision in which school would be best for me. So I would have to say that if it wasn't for my mom, I would still be very confused about my future. I've always been interested in makeup since I was little but I wasn't interested in hair until I was about seventeen. I talked to many people about going to cosmetology school; I talked to people who had already graduated and to people who were still attending cosmetology school. I was always told that it was a tough job and that it takes a while to build a clientele, but I was still determined to pursue this career that I have thought about for years.

When I was little I would always say that I would never be one of those girls who would always have their makeup, nails and hair done and dressed up for absolutely nothing. That changed when I got to high school. I started wearing makeup everywhere and I always had to get my nails done and I found myself constantly trying to look nice no matter where I went. I guess when I got to high school, I felt like I had more freedom and by that time my mom had given up on trying to tell me I shouldn't be wearing makeup.

So after I graduate I plan on going to cosmetology school and getting my cosmetology license. In about ten years, I'm going to try and open my own salon for hair and makeup and strive for success in what I enjoy doing. I've had many people try and talk me out of going to school for hair, but I stuck to what I love and I'm moving forward and doing what makes me happy.

*****

Private Ethan by Ethan Richardson
For thirteen years of one's life, one sits in classrooms and are told to think of what one wants to do in life. It is a question that is asked so often, it is easy for one to simply get tired of it and not give it another thought. This is possibly the worst mistake that one can make in one's life. Once one has decided not to give this question another thought, it makes it difficult to decide when it is time. This is one of the many mistakes that I have made in my life and have

suffered the consequences of it. I have waited until three months out from when my decision has to be made to make up my mind (somewhat). I have pretty well decided that military is the right route for me. I know that many people are going to be reading this and wondering, "What is he thinking?" The simple answer to that is I don't know what I want to do and the armed services could give me some guidance. I also don't feel like college is the right answer for me as I lack the values needed for secondary education. This decision was reached a few months ago, and now I am wrestling with what branch and job I would like to serve in and do.

I am primarily looking at serving in the United States Navy as a HM (Hospital Corpsman). The role of the HM is to provide medical care and support to the fleet, SEALS, Force Recon, and the FMF (Fleet Marine Force). I would ideally like to serve with the FMF as they are the ones going out there and risking their lives for our country. I feel as if that is the least I can do for these men and women, If I stay in for long enough to reach the rate of E-5 (Petty Officer First Class), the I would like to attend IDC (Independent Duty Corpsman) school and be assigned wherever from there. The role of an IDC is a bit more stressful than that of a normal Hospital Corpsman as they are assigned to be the only source of medical care on some of the navy's vessels and units (Submarines, some FMF units, etc). I would like to hold this job because it can translate to civilian work as an EMT, paramedic, or higher in the medical field.

The other branch that I am looking at joining is the United States Army as a Health Care Specialist (Army Field Medic). The role of the medic is similar to that of the Corpsman though the medic will receive EMT-B certification upon completion of their training while the HM will not. An Army medic will most likely see multiple deployments while they are in the service, but this is what appeals to me. After a certain amount of time as a medic, I would like to attend Flight Medic School in which medics are taught the basic principles of medical evacuation. The role of a flight medic is to provide air medical support to wounded soldiers on the battlefield and transport them to hospitals. Holding this job can translate to civilian work as an EMT, Paramedic, or higher in the medical field. Army medics are also qualified to attend Airborne and Ranger School. While this is not something that necessarily interests me, it is nice to be able to keep my options open. Wearing the tab of a Ranger is considered to be a great honor in the Army. It is also possible for medics to move to an 18D MOs, which is a Special Forces medical sergeant.

I became interested in this field of work when my neighbor moved into the house next to ours. He is former Army Airborne and worked as a paramedic and fireman one he was discharged. He said that working as a paramedic can be fun and rewarding but is also challenging. I can remember talking to him about the different things he saw while he worked as a paramedic. Once he was working with a woman when they were called to a wreck. As always, it was lights and sirens all the way there and a serious attitude. It was not until they reached the wreck site that they realized the worst part; one of the fatalities was the woman's mother. He told me this story to demonstrate how it can be rewarding but difficult work. I found that some medics go on to obtain a higher license such as P.A. (Physician's Assistant) or even an M.D. An alternative to this route is to join the South Carolina Army National Guard which would be the same thing except it would be a part time commitment.

My alternative route to either of the military EMS (Emergency Medical Science) careers is at Gaston College. They offer an affordable AAS (Associates in Applied Science) in EMS that will also give the student paramedic certification. It could be beneficial to me to go into the military with this college experience behind me, as well as a paramedic certification. It would allow me to potentially start with an advanced rank as well as make the military medical training easier. It would also give me a work field if I were to decide to not join the military. I would be able to work with many EMS agencies as a full time paramedic. Holding this degree could also help me if I decided to pursue a higher degree in medicine. One of the jobs that I wouldn't mind having later in life would be as a general practitioner. This is a person who practices general medicine and is often your family doctor. This career field has interested me for a while as it is both fun and challenging at the same time. If I chose not to pursue a career as a GP, I would probably look at becoming an ER (Emergency Room) doctor instead.

An AAS entering the military could be useful as it would, with a couple more years of school, allow me to becoming an officer which has a several benefits. One of the most prominent differences between an officer and an enlisted man is the pay scale. The base pay for an officer is close to the pay that someone with years of experience would receive. Officers also receive various other benefits such as their own eating hall as well as the respect that they are given. After twenty years, you would also receive officer's pay for life which is a nice boost at that point from enlisted pay.

I know that some may read this and judge me based on my decisions, and that's ok--you don't have to agree with it. I respect the fact that each and every person has their own individual ideas of what needs to come after high school. I chose to follow the path to becoming a healthcare professional to pursue my own dreams.

*****

The Lessons We Learn by Devin Scott

*"Don't ever let anyone tell you **no**."*

I close my eyes and let the waterbed effortlessly shift my body.
*"Don't ever let anyone tell you **who to be**."*

I roll to one side and exhale a sigh, letting the music...
*"Don't ever let anyone stand in the way of your **success**."*
...drown out the yelling.
*"Don't ever let anyone stand in the way of your **happiness**."*
Happy sixth birthday.

I see a woman I've only known for the first six years of my life. I see a woman who is down on her luck, in and out of jail, with an off and on addiction to meth. I see a woman who's never earned more than minimum wage, never made enough to support herself, let alone a family, and who has never been able to care for her son, no matter how much she longs to.

I see a man I've never seen outside of pictures. I see a man who has been in a dark place, drifting from state to state with a fiery temper and a dangerous alcohol addiction. I see a man who has come a long way in his life, found a new wife, new kids, and a new family, but a man who can't bring up the courage to face his past. I see a man who can't pick up the phone to call his son without crying, because he's fooled himself into thinking that his son can hate a stranger.

I see a boy I've known from the second he was brought into this world. I see a boy who is still writing his own story, and who is still simply brainstorming the plot of his life. I see a boy who has done all he can to learn from other's mistakes, who hasn't run from the past, but embraced it with open arms. I see a boy who has tried his hardest to learn from the past so that it won't be repeated. I see a boy who sees a trail of footprints directly in front of him, but who refuses to follow them, and forges his own path.

I see myself.

"What do you want to be when you get older?" The guidance counselor's question snaps me from my reveries and I lose my staring contest with my reflection in her office window. I turn to her and respond immediately. "I want to be happy." In my mind there's no question, there's no thought, for I already know the answer. She asks, "Well, everyone wants to be happy, but what are you planning to do to achieve that?" What do I "plan" to do to be happy?

Happiness doesn't come from careful planning; it's a state of mind. Life is always going to throw a wrench in our plans, no matter how long we prepare them. Opening our eyes after a restful night's sleep to see the light streaming through the window, illuminating the dust gently drifting through the stale morning air, taking in the sweet but subtle scent of a freshly brewed mug of coffee, the blissfully relaxing feeling we get from our favorite songs resonating within us; the small things are what make life worth living.

"I *plan* to enjoy life as it comes to me, I *plan* to appreciate everything I have while it lasts, I *plan* to spread as much joy as I possibly can, I *plan* to make the world a happier place when I leave than it was when I came in, and I *plan* to enjoy ***every single moment*** of it." I say, voice filled with pride, with a sly grin on my face. "While those are good goals to have, how do you expect to ever accomplish them? Do you plan to go to college and get in public service? Do you plan to get a degree in medicine and save lives? Perhaps you could be a psychologist, or a therapist?" She asks these questions as if trying to garner some response, but judging from her expression she doesn't seem to understand the look of disgust on my face. I'm not disgusted by the idea of going to college, I'm disgusted by the idea that I need to go to college in order to be happy.

There's an old Indian proverb: "When you were born, you cried and the world rejoiced. Live your life so that when you die, the world cries and you rejoice." I can spend my whole life worrying about, and planning to start, a career only to suddenly get hit by a bus and have my life taken from me before it has even started. Or I can start living now. I can take life one moment at a time, and do the best I can to bring joy with every breath I take. I can do my best to have no regrets, and to make every day better than the last, and I don't need a degree to do that.

"I plan to go to college, but that has nothing to do with accomplishing my goals." I say without breaking eye contact, before trying to suppress a chuckle when her face contorts in confusion. "How so?" she asks. "Following the steps to 'success' that are laid out by a traditional education system hardly seems to be in line with my goals. If and when I go to college, it'll be because I want to, not because I need to, and certainly not because I'm told to." I say, punctuating the word "success" with air quotes. "Well, I only ask if you plan to go to college because we need to start preparing now. I don't want to see you close off any doors because your grades aren't up to snuff. I just want to make sure you have the opportunities to achieve what you want," she explains, with a thin veneer of sympathy.

I feel something click in my mind: that's the exact problem with the traditional education system. Grades don't measure intelligence, and they certainly don't measure one's value as a person. Human beings aren't numbers on a page; we're so much more. Each student is a unique individual who learns differently than any other, but students are nonetheless expected to sit down, shut up, and fill out countless mindless worksheets regardless of how well they know the material. Good grades aren't awarded to those who know the material the best, they aren't awarded to those who can put it into practice, they aren't even awarded based on how well the student will fare outside of school, they're awarded to the most obedient students. The ones who don't question the benefit of a certain assignment. The ones who simply do the work.

Students get so caught up in doing the work, and teachers get so caught up in teaching the standards, that we forget what the whole point of education is. To learn. Not to get the best grades, or graduate from the best college, but to learn and better oneself as a person. And it's for this exact reason that I want to be a teacher. I want to do all I can to benefit the youth of the nation, our future leaders, with the best education they can get, and I want to advocate for a reworking of the education standards so that school isn't simply "teach by numbers." I know it will be hard, but there can't be a change without a catalyst. Furthermore, I want to teach history. It's so important for students to understand our failures and shortcomings as a society in order to avoid these same pitfalls in the future. I want to teach that every action ever taken has had consequences, and that every event has had causes and effects. Those who do not learn from the past are doomed to repeat it. I refuse to repeat the past of my parents.

But unlike some people, if I fail to accomplish my career goal, I know I'm not a failure. I don't need a degree or formal job to spread the message that actions have consequences. I'll be the most successful person on the planet if I can only teach people to step back, take a deep breath, and consider their actions. That, and make people smile, which is more important...

"Hello?" the guidance counselor says as she gazes at me inquisitively. "Sorry, I got a bit lost in thought there." I say, attention returning to the conversation. "I'm already achieving my goals, every day of my life. So long as I'm alive, I'm working toward my goals. So long as I'm happy, I'm a success. And so long as I breathe, I won't let anything take that happiness away," I explain, voice swelling with pride. She purses her lips, as though she's holding herself back. I've seen the look enough times to know that she thinks my goals are short-sighted, but she's restraining herself from telling me that I should make new ones. But I know who I am, I know what I want, and I want my goals to be short term, because we can never know where life will take us. As I walk out of her office, I hold my head high because I know that wherever life takes me, whoever I become, I'll be a smiling, shining success.

*****

"It Won't Be Like This for Long" by Emma Smith

Every morning my mom, sister, and I ride to school listening to the local country stations. After bouncing between 96.9 and 103.7, Darius Rucker's song "It Won't Be Like This for Long" comes on the radio. In the song, Darius Rucker sings about his daughter growing up and not needing him like she used to. Every time the lyric "One day soon your little girl is gonna be all grown up and gone," comes on my mom begins to tear up. Until this year, I never really thought about what life would be like when I leave for college or why my mom would always tear up at the thought of me leaving.

When I started high school, I was immediately asked about college and what career I was going to have when I graduated high school. At fourteen years old, I didn't think I needed to worry about what I was going to do when I graduated in four years. Two years later, as I'm finishing my junior year of high school, I've realized that now it is time to decide what I am going to do. From the time I was little, I have always thought I was going to be a teacher. I thought being a teacher would be fun and fairly easy. Boy, was I wrong! After seeing my mom go back to teaching, and all of the work that teaching requires, such as dealing with crazy parents with even crazier kids or grading papers and writing lesson plans for hours on end, I decided I needed to find a new dream.

Now that I was back to square one, I started to think about all of the things I enjoy and find interesting. After watching wedding planning shows and playing wedding and hotel games, I decided that maybe Hospitality or wedding planning would be a fun career. During my sophomore year, I started to research Hospitality careers. Now that I'm a junior, I have decided that this is the path I want to take.

When I graduate, I plan on going to the University of South Carolina Beaufort (USCB) to major in Hospitality or event planning. USCB has a great Hospitality program, and they are even building a new campus on Hilton Head Island for student internships. After studying at USCB, my dream is to intern at Walt Disney World. After vacationing at Disney growing up, I have frequently joked that I would work there after I graduate college because I love it so much. Now that I have to actually start planning for life after I graduate college, I have decided that maybe working at Disney is not really a joke anymore. Disney has a program for students to work in different areas of the park, such as: restaurants, retail, ride operators, and even characters. The coolest job would be to work as a Disney Princess, but you have to meet strict requirements for this job. After going to Disney World with two four year old girls and seeing their faces light up when they got to meet Belle, Ariel, Cinderella, and Merida, I would want to be a part of making a Disney vacation magical by being a Disney Princess. I think the most realistic job would be to work in retail in the parks which will still give me the opportunity to make a Disney vacation magical because of the atmosphere Disney has.

After interning at Disney, my plan is to work for an event planning company. I love seeing people's reactions when their dreams come to life. After graduating, I hope to find a job in the south, preferably between Georgia and North Carolina. I want to live somewhere that is not too far from my family and friends at home, but also somewhere that would give me many opportunities for event planning.

I have considered working for companies such as The Color Run as an event coordinator. After going to The Color Run one year, I think the atmosphere of the company and the event would be fun to work in. I have also considered wedding planning as one of my focuses. After watching *Four Weddings* when it was on TLC, I loved seeing the details and planning that went into these amazing weddings and the reactions that came from the brides. I would like to find one of these jobs or something similar in either Charlotte or Atlanta. I don't think I would enjoy living across the country away from my family in bigger cities like New York City or Los Angeles, where you don't always find southern hospitality. Living in Charlotte or Atlanta will hopefully give me plenty of opportunities to plan events for either large companies or small local companies and still be a quick drive back home.

After living on my own for a while, I hope to be married by the time I am 25. When I am about 27 or 28, I think I will be ready to have kids. I hope to be as amazing as my mom is when I have kids of my own. She always puts me and my sister first, and as a single mom, she works even harder to give us some amazing opportunities. I hope to be able to provide my kids with some of the same experiences and opportunities that my mom has given me.

Now that I have made all of these plans and set all of these goals, it is time to begin to make my dreams a reality. As I think about the past three years of high school, I realize that they have flown by. Right now, I am in the top of my class. and I am taking classes that challenge and push me to do difficult things that I have cried a lot of tears over. I have taken on the challenge of AP US History, and on top of that, my younger sister is in the same class. My sister has always been the smartest one in her class; she was so smart that she skipped eighth grade and moved straight into high school. As a sophomore, she is taking the same classes I am taking as a junior, which at first I wasn't too happy about. Some days I'm still not. In these classes she always gets higher grades than me, and most of the time everybody else in the class. After crying many tears over this, throwing things, and my grandparents saying, "Hun, there's always going to be someone who does something better than you," and me always replying, "Well, I didn't think that someone would always be my little sister!" I have had to make some realizations about myself. I always thought that getting the highest grades and knowing everything meant that you were going to be successful. After being in classes with my sister and seeing how much pressure she puts on herself to make the highest grades and know everything, I have realized that I don't have to be the best at everything I do, and sometimes not knowing something makes for more jokes than always knowing the answers. Also, as I work on these dreams, I get a little scared about what is to come. I am afraid of leaving my family and friends who have always been there for me and helped shape me into the person I am today. I look back on my life and realize that, "It won't be like this for long," and I am trying to soak up every dinner, car ride, vacation, conversation, and adventure I can with my family and friends.

Every year when I go to Michigan with the family that I consider to be my second family, I get asked what I want to do with my life after high school. This year on the twelve hour drive, I believe that I can finally, after five times of being asked that question on the drive, give a confident answer. I believe that this plan and these dreams are attainable and I cannot wait to go on the journey.

Growing up I always dreamed about going to dances, having a locker, driving, and eventually graduating. While I was in class doing crazy amounts of work and trying to make it through the day, I never thought senior year would come. When I would complain about all the work I was doing and how it was never going to end, my grandfather would say, "Hun, you can stand on your head for that long," which was basically the "Pop" way of telling me to stop complaining. Now that my senior year is only a semester away, I've realized that I've "stood on my head" for almost thirteen years. I think about the amazing life I have lived so far, and the ups and downs that I have faced, and I really want time to slow down because "It won't be like this for long."

*****

My Perfectly Glazed Doughnut by Elena Walrod

When I imagine myself in the future, I see a happy woman. In no way do I imagine myself in a certain outfit or with a certain man or even a certain haircut. I see myself smiling or laughing or being my goofy, loveable self. I imagine a perfect summer afternoon, where I am sitting outside on a porch swing, drinking my favorite coffee blend and eating a perfectly glazed doughnut. Or even a cold winter night, where I am laying in my favorite couch spot, snuggled up with my fuzzy blanket and sleepy kitten, watching an overplayed Christmas movie. I imagine a stress-free life. But, like all imaginations, it's not real. It's all in my head. It's all a fantasy. The only person who can make these fantasies come true is me. But how do I make all of my dreams come true? How do I get to the place I want to be? How am I going to get my act together in order to have this "perfect life"? So many questions and about how I plan to live my life in the future. My answer to all of these questions is through happiness.

I remember one summer I was walking with my dad in Freedom Park, and we saw a woman walking her dog. She had tattoos up both of her arms, bright purple hair, and many facial piercings. She wore all black clothing, a band tee, and a baseball cap. After we smiled and passed her, I looked at my dad expecting a reaction. But he continued to walk and smile as normal. So, I asked him, "Did you see her?" He replied, "Yes." "Did you see her hair and her outfit?" I continued to laugh. He replied, "Yes." Still confused as to why my dad wasn't laughing at what ridiculousness we just saw, I asked him, "Don't you think she looked a little CRAZY?!?" I was dying of laughter at this point. All my dad had to say was, "Maybe to you and I, but looking that way is what makes her happy, and we shouldn't laugh at that." My dad's comment stuck with me. Why did I judge the way she looked? I don't want people judging me. From that moment on, I decided to not judge others by what makes them happy, and continue to live my life by doing things that made me happy.

I plan to live my life vigorously and thoroughly. I will enjoy my long nights procrastinating essays, even though that is frowned upon; I will enjoy snuggling my multiple cats, even though I will be made fun of; I will enjoy stuffing my face with my favorite junk foods, even though I will regret it later; I will enjoy getting a tattoo that means something, even though my mother will kill me when she finds out; I will enjoy dancing in my underwear to One Direction, even though I'll be "wasting time"; I will enjoy laughing and crying at the most inappropriate times, even though I'll lose all respect amongst my peers. I plan to live my life through hope instead of regret.

In order to do this, I have to know myself. I need to know what makes me ME. Finding yourself is not a one day project. And I know that these next few years of my life are when I will change the most. There will be life changing decisions that will need to be made. However through all these things, I plan to be myself, whatever that means at the time. Sometimes it will mean crying because I just can't get my college essay to sound the way I want, or sleeping through my spring break because I'm behind on my sleep schedule. Whatever seems natural to me, is what I plan to do.

I realize that the act of happiness and "being myself" does not pay well in the real world. But, my point is not to make a career out of happiness. No matter what college I go to, or what career I have, or what man I marry, I will be happy and make the most out of my life. I will live a positive life no matter what I am doing, or what "path" I take.

I do want to have a full-time job in the future, so when it was time for me to choose my career path, I started off thinking about what made me happy and how I could make a career out of that. I love helping and caring for other people, so I began to look into careers that involved helping others. Eventually, I narrowed it down to two options: social work and physical therapy. Both of these options make me extremely excited for my future, whether it be helping parentless children or caring for a patient.

Even though I have limited knowledge of what the world has to offer, I am confident that I will soak up all the beauty and positivity and use it to my advantage. I want to explore all the beautiful things in the world, whether it is flying to Germany or just visiting a new book store that opened up down the street. Of course, not everything is wonderful and full of life. There is negativity and there is death. I plan to recognize these and learn from them, and help prevent them. In no way will I let the negative or entitled people in the world run my life or take over my happiness.

Now I realize this all sounds extremely optimistic and to most people, impossible. On some days, it even sounds impossible to me. Most of the time, I wake up uncertain about everything. I question how I will even make it through the day without crying or hurting another person I care about. There will be weeks at a time where I feel unsatisfied or unhappy. Not every day will be the best. There will be sleepless nights, ear-splitting arguments, sore legs, unflattering haircuts. But, the second I realize that it is my choice to be happy, and it is my decision to act a certain way towards people, I automatically make the attempt at being in a better mood and acting more appropriately. So, instead of being upset or dwelling on the bad things in life, I will reflect on what happened and learn from it. I will prevent myself from stressing and worrying. Once again, I am confident I can do this, it's in my nature to continue to improve.

So the next time I receive a complicated essay about my future or a simple question about what I see my future like, whether it be from an uptight college professor or a quality friend, I will tell them: "I see myself being happy and eating a perfectly glazed doughnut."

*****

The Pug Life by Rachel Youngblood

I've come a long way in my seventeen years of life. Where do I go next? What is my next step? Most people want to be young forever...they want to party, have sex, do drugs, and drink. I suppose these are fun things to do every now and then, but what's the point in devoting your life to these things? I don't see the point in waking up every morning and smoking before school, smoking after school, drinking and partying every weekend. But I guess that's one of the ways I am different from some of my friends.

I have a year and a half left of high school and all I can think about is graduating. High school has been tough. It has been a lot of late nights doing homework and studying for tests. I have had lots of crazy teachers that are trying to prepare us for college classes and forgetting that we are still in high school. I have lost friends and made new ones. Finally, as a junior in high school, I can say I have some good friends that I feel comfortable being around. I think the main reason I hate high school isn't because I really don't like "high school" but because I don't like school in general. I hate getting out of bed and going to a school full of people who lie to you and talk about you behind your back. Every week I am taught a bunch of things that I probably won't use again in the real world. I guess it's good to know the history of the world and learn about all these great people and their achievements, but do I really need to be tested on my knowledge of these things? I've always liked doing projects that really help me remember this stuff, but I hate studying for hours to memorize stuff just to know it on a test and then not be able to apply it in real life. I'm ready to learn new things that will help me in the future.

I know it'll be scary to be on my own and I'm sure I'll miss being a teenager. I will miss not having responsibilities, being able to eat whatever I want, looking at pictures of pugs for hours, watching YouTube videos and tutorials on makeup looks that I probably won't ever be able to do, and being able to waste time watching the *Rocky* series over and over. Even though I am desperate to be done with high school, I have absolutely no idea what I want to do with my life. I know I want to settle down at a young age and have children young; not young like 18, but young like 25. As for the job thing, I don't really know which direction I'm leaning towards. I once wanted to be an accountant, but in middle school when math started to get harder, that was quickly ruined. Then I started to draw floor plans and realized I wanted to be an architect. But that grew boring and I just stopped doing it. Since then I have thought about being a hairstylist, an interior designer, or a wedding planner. I could be anything I want; I have so many choices. But it scares me that at 18 years old, I will be expected to know what I want to do with my life or where I want to go to college. Every day, different adults ask what I want to be when I grow up, or where do I want to go to college? All I can tell them is that I have goal and that goal is to not have a job that I dread every morning and that I count down each hour until I can leave. I want a job that makes me happy. I also would like a job where the people around me are happy doing their job. Being surrounded with happy people makes me happy.

I have also thought about being a stay-at-home mom. I know that is cliché and women can do so much more now that they used to not be able to do, but I feel like I could be perfectly content cooking and cleaning and spending time with my children. I want to be able to do things with my husband so that our marriage is always strong. I want to always be available to him and my children. Growing up, my mom worked two jobs and if I was sick I had to go to her job with her because she was so consumed with work. A job where I work 40 or more hours a week would potentially put a damper on my relationship with my children and my husband.

One of the main reasons I want to always be available to my kids and husband is so my relationships with them with always be strong. I used to have a good relationship with my mother, but not so much anymore and I haven't had the best relationship with my dad until now. I guess that's one of the reasons it's so easy for me to say I want to be independent. For a majority of my life I already was very independent. I want to always be there for my kids because I never really had that growing up. I guess one of my next steps will be to raise my kids the way my parents raised me with the same morals and values, but at the same time do it better and make sure my kids know I'm not going anywhere.

One of my next steps in life, as a person, will be to get over everything that happened when I was a kid: my parents divorcing, seeing my dad one weekend every month, the constant fighting, having to leave my mom. Parents don't know how hard a divorce is for kids. When my parents got divorced, it was extremely hard to have to go back and forth. One parent got Thanksgiving and the other got Christmas. I always wanted to spend all holidays with my dad so I could be with my older siblings, grandparents, and cousins. It didn't always work out that way, and a lot of times I got really sad for missing out on stuff. I don't want my children to ever have to go through being at different houses for holidays or ever feeling left out. Divorce will not be an option for me. I'm not usually one to give up on something or someone that I have already put a lot of effort in to.

I have a lot to do as a person and a lot of choices to make. I need to be stronger and focus on myself more. I'm gradually getting better at standing up for myself. As for school, after high school I will go to York Tech for two years and give myself time to decide what I want to do. I also think I might need to job shadow some people and maybe that'll help me. I can only hope that four to five years from now I'm a better person and I'm doing something that I love. I also hope that I'll be with someone I love; someone who gets me and knows everything there is to know about me. I picture myself sitting on my couch with my husband, my kids, and my pug watching *Rocky*. I have a lot to do leading up to my next step in life.

THE DREAM

Wet Socks by Austin Ball

As I sit in the mountains of West Virginia reminiscing on a simpler time, I think back to my high school English 4 class when Mrs. DiMatteo had us write a chapter about "The Next Step" in our lives. Since a young age I loved the mountains, and I knew that one day I would hike the Appalachian Trail from start to finish. Now, as I sit by a dimly lit fire that crackles under the midnight sky, I think about what life has been for me since my high school career has ended, and what it may hold for me not only in the near future, but also 50 years from now when I am hardened by many long hours and restless nights, and the "Next Step" will be nearly impossible to reach.

As morning breaks and the sun peeks over the Great Smoky Mountains, the same sky that was once painted a dark, charcoal grey, now resembles a youthful watercolor painting. I think back to when I was sitting in class discussing "The Next Step" in my life. I thought about college, a wife and kids, what career I may have, and an array of things that honestly I could not predict. I did not know what college I was going to attend, whether it be a 4 year university, or a 2 year tech school. Would I get my doctorate and become a great neurologist? Would I get a 2 year business management degree and start a multi-million dollar company? Maybe I'd do neither. I did not know who my wife was going to be, or if I'd ever find the love of my life. Would I ever have kids? Would I be a father of 13, or would my only child be a German shepherd that loved exploring just as much as I did? I was a 17 year old teenage boy who didn't know what life had in store for him, but I had one goal in mind, something that was on the top of my bucket list, and that was to hike the Appalachian Trail.

So I decided the Appalachian Trail is what I'd write about, for it was something that I wanted more than anything and knew for certain I'd make happen. I always talked to my mother about my life dream of conquering the beast of hiking 2,168.1 miles from the hills of Georgia to the mountains of Maine, and every time I brought it up she gave me the same distasteful look. She'd say with the same tone of voice, "Are you trying to kill me Austin Scott Ball? There are murderers on that trail! Are you trying to turn my hair grey?" I'd look at her and laugh, explain to her that the only killers on the trail were either grizzly bears or my own mind. See, for me it was more than just exploring nature, it was about finding out who I truly was, and what better way to find yourself then to spend 6 months of your life with just the bag on your back and God to talk to? Mental toughness would be pushed to its limit, and achieving a personal goal would be greater than words could explain.

As I hike through the Great Smoky Mountains, thousands of trees varying from vibrant shades of green, to warm red-orange surround me. Though most of the leaves have been washed-out from the harsh change in climate, they are still breathtakingly beautiful. As I look at the trees I think about how they're similar to people, because the reality of it is that we are not that different. Trees and humans alike both need water and nutrition to stay strong. We help each other breath and without one another we would not be able to survive. Trees continue to grow until the moment they die, and I find this to be true for people as well. This journey along the Appalachian Trail has helped me grow as a person, not only mentally, but spiritually as well. I am a firm believer that man belongs to Earth, Earth does not belong to man. Enjoying what the Earth has to provide for us had been a wonderful experience and has made me a happier person.

When thinking about what the future has to hold, I do not care about materialistic things. What I truly care about is the people whom I love, and being happy. Happiness cannot be purchased, and true happiness comes from within. To anyone who wants to be happy, I'd say follow your dreams and make them come true. Metaphorically, the next step in my life would be finding Austin. Literally, the next step would be pushing through the dead of winter with soaking wet socks and dealing with the most unbearable blisters that have developed on the inside of my toes and back of my heels. To most people this probably seems like a horrendous idea, but to me it sounds absolutely amazing.

I remember talking to my uncle at one of our family reunions; he told me stories about his adventures as a young man and how he found himself in the years after high school. He bought a motorcycle and told my grandparents that he was off to the Colorado Rockies to become a ski bum. As he left from Ohio on his 1972 Honda Rebel, he only had one thing in mind: finding himself. As he rode through our amazing country he had a lot of time to himself to think about life, and what he'd like to do with it. He hated high school as a kid and had no dreams of going to college--all he wanted to do was adventure. As he reached California he got tired of that small motorcycle and traded it for a bicycle. He then rode his 10 speed all the way up the west coast to Washington, where he decided to work on a fishing vessel. After hard hours and restless nights, he decided that maybe college wouldn't be so bad after all. He went back to Ohio and attended Kent State University and went on to get his master's degree in what he loves. It took him a while to find himself, but now he is very successful and gives credit to those youthful adventures for making him who he is.

Listening to my uncle really inspired me to take time to find myself before I figure out what I want to do in this life. When I mentioned the Appalachian Trail to him, he stated that he regretted never hiking it when he was young because he is too old now and can't physically endure the harsh miles. It occurred to me that I need to follow my dreams before I get too old, so as I sit here by this fire in the mountains of West Virginia, I am thankful that I had that conversation with my uncle. Although I don't want to work on a fishing boat in order to find myself, it made me realize that taking time off between high school and college doesn't mean that you can't be successful in this life.

As a high school student I didn't really know what the "Next Step" of my life was going to be. I liked to think that no matter what happened I'd be happy, and after my uncle told me about his adventures as a young man, and how they prepared him for the next steps in his life, I knew that hiking the Appalachian Trail wasn't going to be a waste of time. The Next Step in my life is a chapter that will write itself, not the one that I wrote in my high school English 4 class. My dad always told me, "If you want to make God laugh, tell him your plans," and I find this to be very true. The truth is that no matter where we think we're going in life, things can always happen and change our future plans. One plan that can't be changed is my decision to be happy, for "The Next Step" can always be a happy one as long as I am content with who I am.

*****

The African Dream by Chloe Craig

As Lo'a Reg laid down that night she had no idea she was about to experience a dream that would change her life forever. A dream that revealed to her a future she had only imagined having. A dream that would be the beginning of her future.

She was finally there! At age twenty-six, all she had been dreaming of her whole entire life was finally coming true. Lo'a Reg had just took her first step off of the airplane and the humidity of Democratic Republic of Congo hit her in the face. But at that moment the humidity was the last thing on her mind. Everything seemed so surreal to her, but she knew she was not there for pleasure: she was on an assignment. She was determined to go and make a pathway for her homeland people who had dreams and visions of being someone and going somewhere, but had no resources to do so. She wanted to give the children who had walked dirt roads barefoot, had swollen bellies from starvation, had never seen a reflection of themselves in a mirror, seven year old children who had to take care of smaller children but still needed someone to take care of them, she wanted to give all of them a chance. A path of hope to let them know that someone out there does care about them, and that is what she was determined to do.

Lo'a Reg grew up in small town Rock Hill, South Carolina, with dreams beyond her reach. There always was a burning passion in her heart to help others, but she knew she had to expand her resources in order to help others. As she was in high school, she began brainstorming ideas to help her develop into a successful entrepreneur so that when she graduate high school she would already have a head start on her future. Her whole family had the desire to own a business, so they decided to start a family business of sending care packages to college students, so that generations to come would have a dependable income. As she continued to work the business, she saved her money over time. She invested her money in different stocks and real estate. She wanted to save enough money so that by age twenty-five she would have enough money to travel and enjoy life freely. But her main goal was to make it to Africa to help people in need.

Her first step to making it to Africa was to begin giving. She was a firm believer in the verse, "Give and it shall be given back unto you" (Luke 6:38). If she was going to help others in another country, she had to help those in need around her first. So she began helping out at soup kitchens, giving her old clothes away to others in need, help build houses with foundations, donating to charities, and just being helpful to others in any way possible.

Loa's next step before making her way to Africa was to travel to all the places she had ever dreamed of going. She wanted to visit Jamaica, Cancun, Barbados, France, and many more. She basically wanted to just enjoy life without the pressure of society telling her how to live it. For example, going to school and graduating, going to college, working a nine to five every day, then working for someone until old enough for retirement. By that time the status of the body may be declining, which prevents an elderly person from enjoying life. She had always told herself at a young age that she was not going to conform to society's way of life and was going to be her own person. So she decided to go and live her life carefree, without any regrets.

After she visited to some of the places she had hoped to travel to, she began to make her way to Africa. She decided to bring along some of her family for support, and to have someone to be with in a place she had never been before. They decided to go to Democratic Republic of Congo because it is known to be one of the poorest countries in Africa. When they first arrived in Democratic Republic of Congo, they went to one of the villages to help out with a food drive. As they were there, they observed the way the people lived, and noticed that mostly everyone there spoke French. Lo'a Reg had taken French classes for the last several months in preparation for her journey. Weeks after being there, Lo'a Reg was able to get books shipped from America to put into the classrooms that were going to be built, so that the children would have a source of education. Later she began to get nurses sent over for the sick people of Democratic Republic of Congo to help them with their health. She had a church built for the religious people of Congo. She had a whole list of things she wanted to do for the people of Africa, and was determined not to leave until those things were accomplished. And after she left Democratic Republic of Congo, she wanted to visit every other country in Africa and do at least one thing for them that would advance their wellbeing.

Lo'a Reg realized as she was traveling to all the different countries of Africa that she had no desire to go back to the United States of America. Her heart's desire was to stay in Africa and live in unity with her people. She moved the rest of her family from America to Africa so that they all could have the opportunity to experience a different side of the world. She had her a home built in Malawi (because the official language is English), and met an African prince by the name of Obasi Agunda who became her husband. As they continued with their lives, Lo'a never forgot her passion to help others in need and always remembered that whatever she did to put God first.

Suddenly Lo'a awoke from her dream, and could not be happier. She began taking the steps that were revealed to her in the dream. She thanked the past for all the lessons, and told the future that she was ready. As Loa' Reg pursued her dreams she always remembered a quote by Mahatma Gandhi, which kept her motivated: "The future depends on what we do in the present."

*****

My Fallout Life by Matthew Culver

Just another day in the town of Sanctuary as I get out of bed and then gently wake my wife. Just as I'm done shaving, she walks up behind me to ask what we're doing today. We take our talk out to the living room where Codsworth, our Mr. Handy Robot, greets us and offers a cup of coffee. Suddenly, I hear our son Shaun start crying, so I dash to check on my son and my wife is following behind me, just in case Shaun needs that motherly touch. After we get him calmed down and changed his diaper, Codsworth beckons me to come into the living room to watch the television.

As I calmly walk in the living room the television is already on and the news anchor is distressed, saying, "The nuclear war has begun," as there are images of bombs being dropped. At that moment, a Vault-tec representative shows up at my door to informing me that my family has been selected to be "dwellers" in the Vault. Without question or debate, I accept his offer of immediately entering the safety of Vault 111.

As my family and I run to the Vault, we see people already crowded at the gate. We push through the crowd to find two men in power armor with miniguns guarding the gate, along with a man with the roster of approved family names. As soon as we are pushed through the gate, we begin our descent into the Vault--and we see the nuclear bomb drop and explode just as we are underground. Everything has happened so fast, but we feel as if we're safe. We talk to the other people in the Vault about what's happening and whether there will be any survivors.

We finally get down to the floor of the Vault and we are greeted by a scientist who tells us we have to be cleansed in a quarantine area, so we enter the pod.

Suddenly, a white vapor starts to come from the top of the chamber and then I black out. I have no idea how long I was unconscious, but I wake up to find myself extremely cold. I can barely see out of the glass, but I look out to see my wife and son in the pod across from me and there is a scientist and an armed man trying to take my son away from my wife. The man has a revolver and is threatening to shoot my wife if she doesn't give the scientist our son. She keeps refusing and the man shoots my wife, the scientist takes my son, and I black out again.

I come to again and then it hits me: I'm freezing cold. I look at the glass and it's completely frozen and then I notice a blinking light with a symbol of a door opening above it. I push on the door to get out and as I do, the warm air hits me at once and I collapse onto the floor. It takes a second or two for me regain control to stand back up; I open my wife's chamber and she is dead. I take the only thing that I can, which is her wedding ring. I find my way around the Vault and I take a lot of 10mm ammo and a matching pistol. I find myself at the vault door but I can't get out without a special key called a pip-boy. I see a body and then a giant roach-creature called a radroach. I shoot, it and then I check the body and find a pip-boy on his arm. I use the pip-boy to get out of the vault and as I rise up the shaft on the platform, the light hits me all at once and blinds me for a second. I look around and there are buildings collapsed everywhere--it's a miracle that some of them were still left standing. As I rummage through the trash and debris, I find my robot Codsworth, who is overjoyed to see me. We go through the town of Sanctuary while Codsworth explains what has happened since I entered the Vault: I was frozen in that chamber for 200 years and there is mass chaos, every man for himself. Codsworth reveals there is a safe haven at a place called Diamond City, and it dawned on me that's the best way to find my son if he is even still alive.

In a few months, I've made it in Diamond City only to find that my son wasn't there. However, I've also helped the Brotherhood of Steel a lot by killing synths that are littered in the Commonwealth. I even stumbled across technology that unlocks teleportation so I go back to the Brotherhood of Steel's Headquarters, which is literally a flying fortress. I offer the technology to one of the lead scientists and within days he has duplicated it so a handpicked group can infiltrate the institution to end this madness once and for all. I was selected as part of the assault group.

We get near the institution and teleport inside. It's a giant factory with Tesla coils everywhere. It's actually breathtaking, but we remember that this is the place where people are making other people into cyborgs otherwise known as synths, and it must be destroyed. We find synths everywhere and it is hard to fight through, but we manage to get to a place that looks like a bedroom.

There he is! My son! I start to talk to him, but he responds negatively and calls out "Father" and then he is shutdown. I was so confused and I went away from the group to find this person called "Father" and as I get to his location, the group does also. I lead the way in and we find a sixty year old man and I ask him what he did with my son Shaun. He looks at me and tells me that HE is my son. He made the synth version of him at a young age because he wanted to create the illusion that I had only been frozen for only 10 years.

After we talk for a little while, I do see a resemblance between us--he looks more like my father, though. Shaun tells me that he plans on nuking all of lower Boston and repopulating the commonwealth with Synths. Now I've come into the hardest choice of my life: should I kill my son in order to let everyone else survive or let Shaun live and let his plan continue? I decide to do the right thing and kill Shaun so that everyone that I've met can survive. We finish destroying the Institute.

The credits finish, I log out and save the game for the last time. Now that I'm finished, the next step that I'm going to take is to go to York Tech and get a degree in Interactive Web Design and Graphics. I would make a couple working websites just for my portfolio. Then I would find a company that needs the help and would be willing to hire someone with little or no experience or find a contract to work on/develop a website. Finally my career would go from there in my job or taking new contracts for websites, But video games will always have a part in my life where I can be adventurous and take totally different steps than the ones I take every day.

*****

To My Future Child(ren) by Morgan Foster

Firstly, I want you to understand how much love I have for you. As I write this I have no idea who you are, how much you weigh, what your grades are, the sports you're interested in, nor who you associate yourself with. I don't know the color of your hair, the shape of your nose, the amount of time you spend getting ready, the spacing of your teeth, nor the sound of your laugh. Although I don't even know your name, I do know one thing; and that is my love for you is unconditional and everlasting. You need to understand that I will always care for you. I will always fight by your side. I will always support you. I will always be proud of you. I will always be your mother and you will always be my child.

Sometimes this unbreakable bond will become strained and it will be hard, but understand I only want the best for you; whatever that may be.

In regards to your uncertainty on your 'next step,' I want you to understand that it's completely acceptable and normal for you to not be certain as to where you're going or what you're going to do with your life. I hope you realize it's not weird to be unsure and you are most certainly not alone in this. Many, including myself, have felt just as you do.

I know that it's hard to imagine your mom as someone your age, but rest assured I'm still dealing with the same anxieties and pressures you're feeling right now. I know the unnecessary amounts of fear and shame caused by a failed test. I know the late night cram sessions and the unquantifiable amounts of energy drinks consumed to survive. I know the dread of not wanting to go to sleep because you felt like you could have accomplished more in that day. And I know the dread of not wanting to wake up because the mere idea of school causes stress and anxiety. I know how easy it is to fall behind and how hard it is to catch up. I know that teachers can sometimes be unfair. I know that just because you do your best does not always mean you're the best in the class. I know that classwork and homework are not necessarily the only important aspects of your educational career; that experiences outside of school can lead to real learning.

And lastly I know the pressure of permanently deciding your future in a few simple questions is simply overbearing. Why do you need to give a final answer so quickly? How does anyone actually expect you to choose a profession when you haven't experienced that job? Should it be based on your interests? What if those interests become boring or change? Should your choice be based on the amount of income? How would you know what actual amount of money you need to live comfortably? What amount to live in excess? Or an amount that isn't quite enough to sustain?

I really wish I had the answers, but sadly I'm still trying to decide myself.

As of right now, I'm a senior in high school. Your grandmother pushed me very hard academically from a young age. I will be graduating a year early because of this intense pressure to be advanced and it has ultimately caused a great deal of stress to befall upon my shoulders. I feel as though I need to be the best in the best field, surrounded by the best people of their respective fields. This idea of perfection has been, both purposely and inadvertently, placed on me and has caused me to lack in self-confidence. It's difficult to imagine myself meeting the standards I feel I'm expected to meet. However, I know that you are not me. You are your own unique individual, with particular triggers that cause stress. Grades may not be what intimidate you or cause you to worry, as they do me. But I do also realize you will inevitably feel inadequate at some point within your life.

But it's important to understand that this fear and self-doubt shouldn't prevent you from doing what truly makes you happy. That is all I want for you. I want you to do something you feel is worth doing. I could care less the title your profession brings, or how much money you receive an hour, nor the amount of schooling needed. If you like what you do than do it.

Unlike many parents, I completely realize and embrace the fact that everyone is their own unique person with unique needs and preferences. I refuse to constrict you into the little box the parents of society have happily built for us. I'm not going to require you to only be a doctor or a lawyer. I don't believe that your profession should be based on the amount of money you make nor the respect your job is expected to have go along with it. I also don't expect you to be a master of the arts or exceptionally creative. You don't have to be an artist or a writer.

Simply put: I want you to be happy. I realize I've said this previously but it is everything that I hope for you. I think it's what every parent truly wants in the end, even if occasionally they believe money, respect, and power equate to happiness. If you are content in your life. If you have found peace in not only your profession, but in your state of being. If you feel as though you are doing what you love for the right reasons. If you are happy, than I believe I have done my job as a parent correctly.

Therefore your 'next step' should always be the one that makes you most happy.

Your Mother,
Morgan

P.S. And at the very least, have good taste in music.

*****

The Fantasy by Danielle Hancock

I've never been someone who plans things out. I just go with the flow. I do think about my future and what it could be like, but I always think, *I'll just see how it plays out. Maybe I'll do this, or I could do this.* I don't like thinking too far into the future, at least not seriously. I may fantasize about how it could be or how I wish it could be. However, it probably won't turn out the way I want it to. For example, I used to always dream of marrying a prince. Oh wait, I still do! Who wouldn't want to marry a prince? I like to be a little bit practical in my fantasies though, so that I can believe it may come true. I've googled princes and looked specifically for their age. I like to learn about them to see if I might actually like them as a person. If he goes hunting every year, then he's not the guy for me. Believe it or not, this is not my favorite fantasy of my future. I want to be an independent woman who works for a living and brings in the money for her family. I guess I'm slowly getting to the point where I'm seriously planning what I want my future to look like, at least, practically. This is my favorite fantasy of my future.

Before I graduate high school, I will get accepted into Clemson, and I'm going to celebrate with family and friends. I will attend the Graduation Formal at my church and look amazing! I'll dance and have a great time. Over the summer, I will start packing my stuff and get ready to go to Clemson. I'll say goodbye to my family and probably cry when I get there. However, I will call them as much as I can and Skype my sister almost every weekend. When I get there, I'll meet my roommate and we will be besties. We will eat at Moe's every day and talk about the cute boys who walk by. We will find a good church to go to and go whenever we can to worship the one true God, because I won't let life get in the way of my relationship with God. I will try to get into the Honors Program at Clemson because if I get accepted into the Honors program, I'm pretty much guaranteed a decent job when I graduate. It will also give me another discount on my tuition. I'll probably date a couple of cute guys to try and figure out what type of guy I like. Right now, I have no idea what kind of guy I like. I won't let a relationship distract me from reaching my goals, however.

I will graduate with amazing grades and go to a medical school in South Carolina. I will intern at a physical therapy office and spend two to four years there. When I am done with medical school, I will look for a good job working with professional athletes, maybe a football team or a basketball team. There, I will meet my future husband. He will get injured and I will help him to recuperate. He will be a great guy, unlike most professional athletes, and we will fall in love. We will date for four or five years and he will propose to me with a white gold ring that has a giant diamond. I will, of course, say yes. We will have a spectacular wedding. Everyone will be there. My sister will be my maid of honor. My mom will be there, looking amazing. My dad will walk me down the aisle. I will wear a ballroom gown so big they have to move the pews over so I can fit through. My wedding gown has to have a pretty long train, also. When my husband and I exchange rings, I will give my dad my purity ring that I have worn since ninth grade. When I have my daddy-daughter dance, my dad will cry. For our honeymoon, my new husband and I will go somewhere fabulous, like Italy, France, Germany, or Bora Bora. We will have an amazing time and when we get back we will move into his mansion and resume with our jobs. We will see each other every night and cook together. We will play video games and act like goofballs together. We will work through all of the tough times together. I will try to be at most of his games. If I am working, I will simply watch it on TV.

A few years later, we will try to have children. I want to have two children: one boy and one girl. I want to be as amazing of a parent as my parents are. They are so great at what they do, it will probably be impossible to be as good as they are. However, they taught me that through God, anything is possible. My husband and I will try to live near my family, specifically my sister. I want to live by my sister so we will stay as close to each other as we are now. I also want our kids to be as close as we are. I will spoil my kids rotten and love them to death. I will teach them about the love of God and tell them about what He has done for me. I will watch them grow up and succeed in life. I'll see them get married and have children of their own. I will grow old with my husband and see my grandchildren as much as I can. I will then die peacefully with the love of my life.

I can only pray that my life turns out as well as this. I know I will have my ups and downs. Life isn't as easy as it seems. I will feel sad, angry, and stressed. However, I will also feel happy and excited. I am afraid of death but it happens. It's a part of life, it's inevitable. I shouldn't be afraid of it. I should embrace it.

*****

I Want to be a Writer…by Kevin Hicks

Whenever someone asks me the much dreaded question, "What do you want to do with your life?," I will usually give them one of two responses. The first, and probably more honest choice, is, "I don't know." The second option, which I will only give if I am feeling confident enough that day in my ability to succeed is, "I want to become a writer." Unfortunately, the ambiguity of that statement leads directly to more questions that usually sound something like, "Well, what do you want to write?," which takes me back to the other response I could have given them for the first question: "I don't know."

Okay, maybe not all of that is exactly true. It would be foolish of me to say that writing is my dream job, while having no idea of what I would like to do or achieve in that field. So, if I had to list my top three career choices, they would be television writer, novelist, and journalist, in that order. All I really know is that I would like to have a job where I am encouraged to think freely and share my ideas and opinions with the world, rather than perform the same tasks every day.

When my future self sits down to write his collection of memoirs (because his life story will be so interesting that it requires multiple volumes), part one, which would be the chapters surrounding childhood and adolescence, will end almost immediately after I walk across the stage at high school graduation. I find it it hard to believe that this huge milestone is currently only one more year away. Part two would begin with the summer before college. With any luck (and money, of course), it will contain at least some travel across the United States so I can experience what life is like away from the east coast. I will return to South Carolina that fall for college, and I will hopefully attend Winthrop University; though I have not yet decided whether to major in Creative Writing or Mass Communications.

My future self will detail in many, many pages his college experience. He will tell of the agonizing struggle of writing so many essays, the hearts he shattered, and the crazy, wild… studying… he did in order to maintain decent grades. Four years of that necessary torture will go by, and college graduation will come. He would then write about adjusting to life in the big city (either Los Angeles or New York City— I have not yet decided), which is where he moved afterwards. Life in not-Rock Hill, South Carolina is full of writing opportunities and cute guys, which is exactly what future Kevin's former self (basically me in this moment) always dreamed of. After gaining some experience in the TV industry and maybe one or two more broken hearts, my dreams of having my own series be picked up by a network and of becoming engaged to my boyfriend would come true. This would be the end of part two, the next step in my life.

But of course, the future is uncertain and unpredictable. There are an infinite amount of endless possibilities, and just knowing that terrifies me. The next step that I hope my future self will write about someday is nothing more than a dream I have, and one that will likely never come true. Not because it is impossible, but because I am scared to fail at something I have wanted so badly for so long. To avoid failure, I may never even attempt to become that writer on television or that best-selling novelist. I could just graduate from high school, never go to college, and keep my current job as a Quality Assurance Associate (fancy title for a janitor, right?) at Food Lion for the rest of my life. I'm sure it would guarantee me a safe and comfortable life financially, but then I would always regret not following that dream I once had, but probably still would have.

When I think of my next step from this moment, I think of a time that is going to last for at least the decade. There is a lot I would like to do during that time aside from college and working. When I take off on my post-high school expedition, it would most likely be a road trip to places across the United States (and to a lesser extent, Canada). I would visit cities such as San Francisco (because it is virtually the gay capital of America), Los Angeles (because that is where most television networks are headquartered), Nashville (because of the music and the cute guys with their cowboy boots, guitars, and big dreams) and New York City (because it is NYC, the Big Apple, for crying out loud!). These are all places I have never been, but would really like to get to someday. The sooner that day comes, the better. As for international travel, those vacations can wait until after college, I suppose. Vietnam, New Zealand, and the Seychelles are my three most desired places to travel to.

Aside from wanting to travel the world, I would also like to become an inspiration to someone during the next step in my life. After I have found a steady job on television where my name is in the credits of some show regularly, or I have a publishing deal to write and release novels frequently, or I find employment at a newspaper company somewhere, all I ask is that just one person in this world of over seven billion people, finds me to be inspiring. Someone would see me— an openly gay black man— living the successful life of his dreams in this heteronormative and racist world. Doing just that calls for a round of applause, don't you think?

My future certainly is nothing but a mystery. It could turn out exactly as I hoped it would, or my life could end up being dramatically different in either positive or negative ways. I guess it all depends on how much effort I am willing to put in to make my dreams and more come true. I would like to say that I'll just sit back and watch the story of my life unfold, but nothing would ever happen if that is the way I intend to live my life. Moments of the future have already arrived since I started writing this piece, and there is so much more future yet to come. Though I am a bit nervous about the dramatic changes coming my way in a year's time, I am ready to close this current chapter in my life, and begin a new one.

*****

Dreaming of a New Future by Meghan Joseph

When I was fifteen, I used to love going to Carowinds every day in the summer. They had good food, a variety of rides, and a waterpark--it couldn't get better than that. My friends and I would always go and stay a long time.
Carowinds was expensive, but if you had a season pass you only had to pay once! We planned on going to the waterpark on this day, but before we went we wanted to squeeze in a few rides. While in the long line for "Boo Blasters," it felt like it honestly might have been a thousand degrees outside.
My friends and I used to joke about passing out due to how hot it was, but it never actually happened, until that day. I began telling my friends I felt lightheaded, and in mid-sentence, I unexpectedly fell over. I remember blacking out, but still being able to hear people screaming and shouting. I hit my head fairly hard when I fell.

When I came to, I noticed I was lying in the grass. It wasn't just any grass--I was in the quad at Winthrop University. I didn't remember what happened, but I do know that I shouldn't have been at Winthrop. I got up and began to walk around and noticed that I didn't recognize any of these students. I roamed the hallways and peeped in the windows of all the classes. I couldn't help but notice one of the girls in the last classroom looked a lot like me. I only saw her from behind, but she still resembled me. I waited until that class ended and saw her walking out. I finally saw her from the front and I was right: she was an exact replica of me, only a little older. I tried to get to her fast to get to the bottom of this confusion, but she was in a hurry. I decided that talking to her would only make things worse, so I continued to watch her from afar. I noticed she worked really hard, which was way different from my work ethic in high school. It then came to me that I was visiting my future. And I realized that I would have to work hard in order to keep my future the same. This was almost like a wakeup call. It was showing me how bright my future could be if I just stay motivated and work hard.

After a while of watching my future self, I finally woke up and came back to reality in a hospital room. My mom was asking me a bunch of questions but all I could think about was my future. It turns out I had a minor concussion from hitting my head when I passed out, but the doctor said I should be fine, even though I had to wear a weird bandage on my head.

For a while, all I could think about was my life after high school. I was very excited to see what else my future would bring. I completely changed my work ethic along with my whole outlook on school. I realized it was just something I would have to complete in order to move on and have a good life. My grades started to change miraculously; my teachers were very impressed and pleased. I started to take my ACT and SAT scores way more seriously. I took a bunch of practice tests, looked at the practice booklets, and took a one-on-one prep class. I did everything possible to make sure that my test scores were good enough.

I realize that prior to my accident, I was at risk of both being lazy and settling for the future that came after that. Now I have a new attitude that will help me realize how important it is to stay motivated and never lose focus. You have to keep your eye on the prize no matter what that prize is, and you can never give up or settle. Settling is the worst thing you can do, along with being lazy.

This last year of high school should fly by if I don't continue to fool around. I'd never passed out before or anything close to it, but in a way I'm glad I did. If I hadn't I wouldn't have learned the valuable lessons I did. I hope I can do everything it takes to make sure that my future ends up the way I saw it n my dream. I might not attend Winthrop University, but I at least want to go to some nice college. I haven't quite got my eye on any right now. But I can guarantee you that that's all I'm going to be focused on from now until graduation.

*****

I Will by Max Kennington

Everyone has a future. Some people feel like they have it all planned out, while others feel lost in a sea of the unknown and have no idea what their futures will be like. Time will inevitably go on, so even though I may be unprepared myself, I like to think I have it all figured out.

I will graduate from York Preparatory Academy in May of 2017 in the top five of my class. Senior year is gonna be great too--I'm still going to have all of my friends and everyone will be sad to see me go. Mrs. DiMatteo will greet me as I walk the stage and her final words to me will be, "You did good, kid; you did good." And with a tear in my eye, I'll tell her that she helped me along the way, and for that I am forever grateful. I'll come off the stage and see all my friends who graduated in 2016 and came to see the class of 2017 graduate. No one has any hard feelings anymore and we are all friends again. After I talk with them, I see my parents. They tell me how proud they are, how far I've come, and how far I can go. I will believe every word of it, too.

My first day at college, I will walk through the gates of Clemson University (in my dream, Clemson has huge gates). I'll keep the same thoughts running through my head: the girls are going to be beautiful, the classes are going to challenge me, and everyone's going to like me. I will go to my dorm to meet my roommate, and he will eventually become my best friend. We will have a lot in common and he will always be there for me when I need him. I will do well in all of my college courses, while still maintaining a social life and a solid sleep schedule. Freshman year will be a breeze, and sophomore year will be just as fun. Then, junior year will be the best year of my life. I will be at the peak of success with my courses, and I will meet the girl of my dreams. We will meet at a party, and I'll think she's the most beautiful girl that I've ever seen. Vanessa Vasquez will love me, and I will love her. Then, senior year comes around. My grades will still be good, my girlfriend will be even better, and future me will be ready to start his life in the real world. I will graduate high in my class, and then get my Masters of Business Administration. This will require me to stay an extra two years in college, and Vanessa will find a small apartment near the campus so that I can still see her often.

A year out of college, Vanessa and I will travel the world. Her parents will be quite wealthy, and she will want to travel and bring me along. We will go to Italy, France, Germany; we will even hike Mount Everest. One of our trips together will be to Niagara Falls. There on a boat, as a rainbow is posed ahead of us, I will get on one knee and ask the woman of my dreams to marry me. She will say yes, and the entire boat will say, "Awww! So cute!" When we get back to South Carolina, I will get a job. I will manage a large company, and be paid a large salary. While I'm at work, Vanessa will be planning our wedding and making it just perfect. We will live in an apartment until I am able to get Vanessa the house that she deserves.

I will get married on the first of May in 2025 to the woman of my dreams. Soon after the wedding, I will surprise her with our own house, a house that is right on the lake. Everything will be perfect. A couple of months into our marriage, we will conceive a child--a baby boy that we will name Parker Chadwick Kennington. He will be the cutest thing in the whole world, and he will look just like his mother. Vanessa will want to have another child, a baby girl. So, a few months will go by, and Jennifer Lee Kennington will be born. She will want to go by Jenny, and she will get her looks from her father.

I will get old. Time is inevitable, and I will never be immune to its effects. At the ripe old age of 78, Vanessa will breathe her last breath. My kids are now having kids, and their lives are amazing and all planned out. The heartbreak the love of my life will slowly kill me from the inside out, until ame year that Vanessa dies, I will take my last breath. My funeral in Rock Hill, where it all began. All of my friends from high school will be there, and my roommate from college. My children and their kids will be there. The day will be dreary and the night will be cold. My tombstone will read: "R.I.P. to the man who had it all planned out: William Maxwell Kennington."

Life is going to happen. Nothing that I can do or that you can do will make it stop. So even if you don't have a plan for the future, you can still have a dream. This was my dream. The perfect life. I have no idea what my future actually holds for me, but I can only hope that it goes a little something like that.

*****

Mid-life Contemplation by Jake Lowman

In the midst of a deep and wholesome sleep, a loud and not pleasant sound came from my alarm clock, waking me for a new yet delightful day.

My name is Jake Lowman, I'm a 45 year old man with a beautiful wife and three wonderful but aggravating children. I start my day by walking...no, trying to walk to the bathroom to put my contacts in so I can start my day. After struggling to get them properly fitted, I take my morning shower to wash the night off and begin a great new day. Once finished I brush my teeth, fix my hair, get dressed, and finally walk down stairs to see my lovely wife cooking me breakfast: bacon, grits, and toast, my favorite. Once I sit down she greets me with a cup of coffee, a "Good morning sweetheart," and a kiss on the forehead. I say to her that I'm truly blessed to have a wonderful wife like her. She blushes then sets my plate of food down in front of me. We have our morning talk and discuss how each of our days might go. She says she is excited to take our daughter to her first day of kindergarten and then take our two sons off to their schools. I'm an extremely excited parent to witness my beautiful and sweet daughter begin a new chapter of her life. just then, my middle son Alex runs in saying that his older brother thad hasn't got out of the bathroom in almost twenty minutes. I walk up there and say through the door, "Thad, it's time to hurry up! Other people in this house need to get ready also." He grudgingly walks out and says, "Fine. There, Alex, it's all yours." These kids are going to drive me insane, but I can't help but love them. I turn to Thad and say, "I know you need time, but others need time also." The more I pound into my children's head that they have to respect each other, the better off they will be. I look down at the time and realize it is time to leave for work, so I give both my sons a high five and an "I love you," then I give my daughter a hug and a short pep talk about how proud I am of her for starting her new school, and finally I rush downstairs to my wife, give her a kiss, and say that I hope she has a great day.

I slip my boots on and dash for my work truck. Having to get to a jobsite that is 35 minutes away when I only have 20 to get there will be difficult, but I can probably make it. As I'm rushing through traffic, I call my boss to tell him I have the line switching procedures completed and ready to turn in. At Duke Energy, safety and communication between people is required and strictly mandated. I manage to pull in right on time to meet the other relay technical engineers I will be working with today. It will be a crew of four guys, including myself, who will be fixing, or at least trying to fix, a fault in a 100 watt line. A heavy storm caused a tree to fall on it, thus shutting off power to one of our biggest customers and countless residential homes. a big and daunting task is before us. First we will cut off receiving and outgoing power from the closest substations, providing us a safe working environment. Then we will properly fix any and all faults, (loose connections or breaks) in the line. Lastly, we will go to both substations and reboot and reprogram the circuit boards and transformers. By the plans and instructions, it seems simple enough, but it is not. Relay technical engineers deal with very high voltages that can kill faster than a blink of an eye. Once the power coming and going is shut off I begin the job of fixing the damages at the substations. While my co-workers call and make plans with linemen to fix and damages in the lines that were broken. This task is very difficult and mistakes are not allowed. If I, or any of the people I'm working with, make a mistake, it could cost hundreds of thousands of dollars and potentially knock off power to entire cities, counties, or states. Time is crucial but necessary to fix a problem this big and devastating. This project will take days to fix but my job should only take a day to fix. After going to both substations and shutting off power the linemen start their job or repairing the line while me and the crew of relay tech begin to reprogram and fix the transformers and circuits. If any mistakes are made, whole machines costing upwards of five hundred thousand dollars can be ruined. Once reprogrammed and all problems are recorded and documented, we must call our personal bosses and tell them step by step what we fixed and repaired. Lastly we then call TTC (transmission control) and tell them the same step by step process and see if we made any mistakes by us both testing all equipment and machines used in our repair and maintenance for the day.

After double and triple testing all equipment used my day's work is completed, I can finally start my journey back home. After logging over 200 miles of traveling in a day I am more than enthusiastic to be home to a warm meal by my beautiful wife. At supper I ask my family how their day was. Thad was excited he got a B on a test he and I studied multiple hours on. Alex is right at the age of beginning to like girls, so that was all he talked about. Oh, how I remember the days of being a teenager and the slight independence I felt and loved it! Next my wife tells me how stressful her day was, but she still managed to smile through it all. I can only wonder how lucky I am to be her man. She works as a gym teacher and athletic director and coordinator at the local high school. Even though her job is stressful, she does it with a willingly and kind heart. She loves to work with children and help them grow into better people in society. She is a true blessing to not only me but our entire family. Lastly, I ask my daughter Winter how her first day of kindergarten was. She was so excited to tell me what she learned and what new friends she made. I can only imagine what bright ideas will come from her mind. After supper the boys and I clean everything up and head out to our auxiliary garage where our man toys are held.

I have a true passion for older cars and trucks. I try my best to pass on my love for cars to my children who seem to be very interested in them as well. Thad is driving a 1972 CST and Super Cheyenne Chevy Blazer we all restored for him. I drove one in my high school days and I want him to have the same awesome memories in it as I did. We restored every nut and bolt on it. We also did a few modifications to it, such as a built 454 big block engine, 5 speed transmission, 6 inch lift, 36 inch boggers, and true dual exhaust. He wanted it to be factory medium blue with white accents. He and everyone else who sees it falls in love with it! Alex is more of a car guy; he caught his eye on a 1968 Chevy Camaro RS. As you can tell, we are a Chevy family. We have done most of the restoration to it. He wanted a black cherry paint color with silver metallic flakes in it. The car is stunning to see in person. We put a 383 stroker motor in it, a supercharger, 5 speed manual transmission, 14 inch wilwood disk brakes and made it from a hardtop to a convertible. He will be able to drive soon and he cannot wait to start driving this beauty everywhere. As for myself, my sons and I are putting together a 1971 Dodge Challenger manual with a 440. I love teaching my sons the knowledge of cars and working on them. They see it now as boring time with dad, but one day they will do this exact same thing with their children and cherish these moments as I do. After we stay up well past their bedtimes, I take them inside and put them to bed. Then I make my way to bed and fall asleep, looking forward to waking up to another day like this one.

I hope my life will continue to be this amazing with my beautiful wife and children. We love spending family time together at home or out doing something. In today's society, families are so separated and I hope to change that with mine. I've heard my whole life that the family that plays and prays together, stays together, and I believe that to a point. I love this chapter of my life but my next step is to become a grey-headed man sitting in a rocking chair holding hands with my still beautiful wife, talking to all my grandchildren. Some are in high school and some are just beginning their lives. As they gather around, I tell about my past and fond memories. One distinct memory I tell is about how important high school is. I recalled a fond memory about an essay I did in my English IV class. I had to write about my next step and my future. I wrote about how I wanted to live my life and hopefully be important to a job and a family one day. I enjoyed writing it and I showed them the paper I wrote. I told them that they will have to understand and figure out their own next steps towards their own futures. My next step right now is scary, because

I come even closer to death and its challenges. As the days become harder to overcome, I know because of the love and affection I showed my family and now their families, that they will show the same to me. I close with a final word: each day is a new chapter, live it to the fullest and always be happy.

*****

The Sound of My Music by Sam McCloud

My dream, since I was young, was to be in the spotlight. I would always imagine myself famous doing entertainment. Either I would want to be a comedian, music producer, a rap artist, radio talk show host, or just all of those professions. When I first started getting into a certain artist's music and looking at music videos and interviews, I told myself I want to do that, too. I want to live that life, and become a part of the entertainment world.

I started making album art and songlists for artists I like just for the fun of it. In later years, I started to have an interest in the piano and the bass guitar. So I bought a cheap keyboard and taught myself how to play. Then my parents got me a bass guitar and I taught myself that instrument, too. The special thing about me playing the guitar and the piano is that I play by ear. I would look up a song I like, then I would just sit and listen and try to mimic the sounds in the song. I would also go on Youtube, and search up piano tutorials on songs I like. During that process I wouldn't really see what the notes the instructor of the video would play, I would just see where they would place their fingers and just listen to the sound.

I am always the person to enjoy the sight of someone laughing or smiling at what I tell them. I really love making jokes and making someone laugh. The feeling that it brings me is indescribable. Before I got to high school, I was really shy and didn't want to communicate with the other kids at my school; I was pretty much a loner. When I got more mature and actually made friends and hung out with people more, I got more comfortable with expressing myself and showing my feelings. I would tell my friends stories and things that happened to me with other friends, and my friends would laugh. They liked the way I would tell the funny stories and how I can bring up another joke to keep them laughing. I first got the inspiration and thought of being a comedian when my best friend Darius, told me that I would make a great comedy man. I thought to myself, "Maybe that would be a cool thing to think about." I started to look and stand-up comedians that I thought were my kind of style of telling jokes. The more I watched other comedians; the more I experience more stuff in my life. And the more people I made laugh they'd want me to tell the same story again.

Now imagine this: in my dream I'm on stage performing at a concert. I see that I'm with my friends, on the stage in front of a huge crowd. Everyone is going crazy to the beat of the song I'm performing. They all are chanting my name, asking for an encore. The vibe and energy is perfect as I smile to the crowd.

I always had the dream of getting famous off of rapping and performing and shows. The real reason I want to be a rapper is to meet other famous artists I look up to. I like to rap because I like how things sound when you rhyme words together. If I had a choice to talk any way I wanted, I would want to rhyme every time I spoke. I started getting the thought of getting into a rap career, when my mom used to let me listen to old hip hop artists that she used to listen to. She introduced me to A Tribe Called Quest, KRS-1, Run DMC, Wu-Tang Clan, Slick Rick, Public Enemy, N.W.A...basically any artist of the 80's or 90's. After I had knowledge of artists like those and paid attention to how they sound when the rhyme, I started looking at hip hop artists that don't have their music played on the radio. Artists like: MF Doom, Quasimoto, Tyler The Creator, Odd Future, KMD, Casey Veggies, MC Paul Barman, Bishop Nehru, Earl Sweatshirt, Childish Gambino, Captain Murphy, and Chance The Rapper. Afterwards, I saw how much fun my favorite rap artists were having doing what they like to do, I was like, "I want to do that and have fun with it." So during freshman and sophomore year, I wanted to start a collective hip hop group. My little brother came up with the name: Young Twisted Panda Force (YTPF), and my best friend Darius, Nolan, and Chazz were in the group with me. At the age of fifteen, I recorded my first song at Nolan's house. The song I recorded was called "Lucy." At first when I finished the song and listened to it, I liked what I did. Nolan decided to write my part for me, because he knew it was my first time and he was more experienced than me in rapping. The song was basically a love story that I didn't want to do because I hate love story-type things, but I just wanted to test my skills. I decide to make a Soundcloud account and post my first single on Soundcloud. I got older and realized (in my opinion) that the song "Lucy" wasn't good--it was horrible. During junior year and now as a senior, I started recording better stuff and I picked up the idea of making music--as in producing and mixing music. My group and I started getting our music out and letting our peers listen to us on Youtube and Soundcloud, and they liked us. I started getting noticed more and I made more friends and fans in the process. We were mentioned in the school's newspaper, talking about new talent related to music. So, basically YTPF got school, or Rock Hill, famous.

After that, I broke up the group and thought it would be better for me to work by myself for a while and really focus on my music production. Since YTPF, I've had multiple people reach out to me, asking me to make a beat for them or asking if I would write for them. I would always turn them down, because I just wanted to work for myself and not deal with other people trying to be a musician or just mainly groups in general. Currently, I'm ready to try the whole music group type of thing again. But I don't want to make a rap group anymore, I'm more into neo-soul now. I choose to do a neo-soul group, because I started listening to people like The Internet, Milky Wayv, Flying

Lotus, Thundercat, Kilo Kish, and Jameel Bruner. Now I'm trying to organize my soon to be group and the name I'm giving it is called "The Kool." I want to include my friends at YPA like Elaine, Nia, Eric, and probably my former YTPF members. So that's what I want to do with my life and I seem excited and too hyped, for my friends and family I do this, and I'm trying to everything on this list. I do this.

> Imma find my wings like Tyler The Creator,
> and tell you a poem like I'm doing you a favor.
> I'm old school, dap you up like I'm your uncle,
> face the facts it's a cycle. Got caught up in
> the crowd so I guess I'm so crazy, Sam is the man
> so I guess I'm so wavy. Lazy rapper doing this for
> laughter, Imma be watching my pockets getting fatter
> so what's the matter. I hail from the West Coast
> like the greats, all I need to do for my dreams is chase
> and wait.

Patience is key.

*****

The Future Is Mine by Maia Morrison

My future is one of the scariest things I've ever had to think about. The most nerve-wracking part about my future is the fact that it is mine! My future can't be found in a search engine or defined by a dictionary. *My future*. Two words that can't be interpreted by anyone but myself. Two words that depend solely on my actions and reactions.

I have begun to realize that I have yet to begin my life: everything up until now has been practice, as if I've been trapped in a cage and the key is slowly turning in the lock. The part of my future I am most anticipating is my freedom. I think my future will be superior to my past and present because of the amount of freedom I will have. Without the ability to dream and explore life for myself, I don't think I will have enough determination to begin my own business or to achieve any of my other life goals.

Malcolm X once said, "Education is the passport for the future, for tomorrow belongs to those who prepare for it today." To his admirers Malcolm X was a courageous advocate for the rights of blacks, but fault-finders accused him of preaching racism and violence. He has been called one of the greatest and most influential African Americans in history. In the future I hope to be seen as influential and esteemed, and maybe even controversial, like Malcolm X.

In my generation, I think that education is one of the most under-appreciated gifts. We've all wanted to punch a wall because of a bad test grade, or cried at 2 in the morning because of an all-nighter that wasn't worth it, but education is a fundamental part of our lives. Without an education, many of us would have to live off of a mediocre salary and constantly need assistance from those who are more educated than us. If our educations were erased, or greatly diminished, our overall lives would suffer tremendously. Without an education, my career goals would be virtually impossible.

Although my future audience may not be as broad as Malcolm's was, I hope the effect I have on others' lives is as substantial. I want to help those in pain, whether physical or emotional, by attending a two-year college to work toward attaining my Bachelor's in Business. From there I see myself transferring to a four-year college to finish my degree. I am hopeful my next step will be going to a school for massage therapy or learning more about counseling. I have not yet determined whether I want to counsel children or those in failing relationships.

If, for some reason, I cannot become a massage therapist or counselor I want to be a chef. I would love to own a small diner in or near Charlotte, North Carolina. Many restaurants throw away pounds of food every day instead of helping those in need! If I were a chef I would go to every restaurant I could and find a way to save all of the leftovers for the homeless. At my own restaurant I hope to help the homeless every weekend with free food and a place to lay their heads.

If none of my realistic career goals are attainable within five years I want to become an actress, singer, or comedian. I've always had a passion for singing, acting, and making others laugh. Although these careers are all somewhat impractical, I think I have what it takes to become successful in each field. If I became famous I would use my fame to help others by donating a large portion of my profits and time to those in need. I would love to help find cures for diseases like cancer, HIV, and diabetes.

I would also love to be a plus sized model. I haven't thought much about this plan, since it's my most outrageous one. Although I am not extremely confident with my body image, I would love to be an example for other girls. Since middle school I've experienced diffidence and timidity because of my outward appearance. Like many others in my shoes, I've used my personality to distract myself from my occasional negative thoughts. I would love to help others see themselves in a different light without masking their problems or being arrogant.

In fifty years, I hope to retire and use my savings to travel to Hawaii. My mother was born and raised in Hawaii, but when she left for college at age eighteen, she never looked back. I pray that I can meet some of my mother's surviving family members and create a bond with them that I've never had with my stepfather's family. I also hope to eventually travel to Maryland, where I was born, and possibly move there permanently.

Another inspiring quote for the future is, "Don't tell people your dreams--show them!" I found this quote inspirational because it's very realistic. Sometimes we are so eager to tell people about our plans for the future that we get discouraged when they tell us doubtful things. Many of us see ourselves moving places and achieving goals that others think are impossible. I have experienced skepticism before and it isn't an easy thing to "bounce back" from because skepticism from others can fill us with doubt and worry, and keep us from reaching for our goals.

For anyone still reading, I have one final piece of advice. Your future is yours and you may do with it whatever you want! However, your past and present are also yours. Every detail, every bit of them are yours, and you should behave as such. We will all make mistakes and do things that we regret, but those things should never hold us back from bettering our lives. Look at your mistakes as broken pens that have run out of ink and your present as a brand new pen. Will you only mark out your old mistakes with that brand new pen, or will you start another astounding chapter?

*****

Hello, Little Me by Elaine Moses

Hello Little Me, come sit and listen for a while. I have so much to tell you. From your first car, first crush, first heartbreak, and your first accomplishment. I know I'm still young and learning new things at the age of 18. I'm sure there will be problems I will soon have to face in the future and learn from, but I promise it will be filled with light and joy. Right now, Little Me, you are six years old and will have to learn how to grow on your own. But I want to give you a head start for what's coming next.

Growing up, you will wish that someone could just hand you a booklet filled with information on what to do in life, and how to do it. This may sound scary, but Mommy and Daddy won't always be there to protect us. Right now they are trying to keep you from all the bad things of the world. Until one day you'll want to explore for your own and learn the hard way. They will try to guide us, but let's face it, you and I both know that we are too stubborn and headstrong to cooperate for too long. Our mind is easily distracted, yet we can either let that be our weakness or our strength.

We have the ability to see both sides of a story without choosing what's right or wrong. We will want to understand what makes the world and the people in it tick.

With our mother's firecracker attitude, imagination, and our father's huge heart, and strong will, they have created a spontaneous and imaginative daughter.

Growing up you'll ask yourself, "Why don't people understand me? Why is the world the way it is? How can people be simple minded? What is considered normal? What is normal? How can I change the world?"

Your head will be filled with ideas and wonders about the world. This is what makes you so curious and bold about life. You will always want to open up the depths of the universe and read it like a book just to know exactly how it *ticks*. And with this curiosity you will turn to books for information. There you find that you have an interest in the fictional world of pages created by unique writers.

As you travel through air or car to visit Grandma and Papa in California, your arms will no longer be filled with Barbies or Bratz dolls. Soon your little arms will filled with chapter books, like *Junie B. Jones, The Magic Tree House,* and *Captain Underpants.* You won't really care for pictures; the more words the better. You'll want to soak it all in like a dry, eager sponge.

But, Little Me, you will face some judgment at a young age. Since you are too little, you won't catch it, but it will stick to your memory as a reminder to chase your dreams and push your ideas to the limit. Living here in Wisconsin, you will be underestimated by your Language Arts teacher. He will judge your education based on our skin color. The teachers of your first grade will send you to a *special* class to help you catch up with the other classmates.

I want you to listen to me carefully Little Me; don't let *anyone* tell you that you can't accomplish the impossible.

By the time you move down here to South Carolina, in a little town called Rock Hill, the teachers won't believe how bright you are. In the second grade you will read at a fifth grade level. And the more books you feed to that little mind of yours, the more ideas begin to form in your head.

Carefully, Little Me snuggles closer in my arms and looks at me with wonder in her brown eyes. I know that look all too well, just when her lips part to form a question. "What's going to happen with all these ideas in our head? How will they get out if they are locked up inside us?"

I simply smile and say, "We write."

I tell Little Me about all the journals we kept hidden away under our bed. Pages upon pages will be filled with fictional tales. First it will start off as just a small hobby. But soon it will turn into something that we truly love and have a passion for. Wherever you travel a pen and notebook will be in hand, along with a few books.

By your freshman year of high school, others will become interested in what you write. It may be uncomfortable at first, but the more people who start to enjoy what you write, the more confident you will be.

In the tenth grade, you will want to let your work become public for *all* to read. That is when you become introduced to an app called Wattpad. It's a place where all creative writers can allow others to read their stories. The first book you 'publish' will get over a thousand views and votes after two months. The feedback and votes from those readers will motivate you to continue writing. Which brings me to now, in the twelfth grade.

Now, as a senior, you already know what you want to major in. You've known it all your life growing up, but it was never a big deal to you. Soon we will want to become one of the greats like James Patterson, Stephen King, Stephenie Meyer, Edgar Allen Poe, and even Mary Shelley. All have their own style of writing, which is exactly what we plan to do as our next step in life. We want to create our own unique style and share it with the world. It is our dream to touch each and every reader individually with our words. Whether it be bad, good, or sad, we want to leave our readers with a strong emotions like John Green did in his well-known book, *The Fault in Our Stars*.

That is why we want to go to college to learn more about how to become a great writer. I know there may be challenges along the way that will make us almost want to quit, but the fire in our heart that our mom gave to us will never burn out. And with our open mind and kind heart, we will take the criticism like a champ and learn from our mistakes without getting upset. In the end, I know our hard work will pay off.

Who knows, Little Me, maybe one day our books will inspire someone with the passion and desire to write just like us. Soon we, too, can be on *their* list of greats. But until then, keep dreaming, Little Me.

We will one day change the world with just a pen and paper.

*****

Call Me Sam by Hannah Smith

INT: Dress shop
A woman is standing in a prom dress store looking at prom dresses. She is probably in her mid-forties. Meanwhile, her daughter is in the dressing room, reluctantly changing into a bright pink poofy dress.
MOTHER: Come on out Samantha. You've been in there for forever.
SAM: *(steps out in dress and looks in mirror)* I told you to call me Sam.
MOTHER: OHH! YOU LOOK SO ADORABLE!
SAM: I look like a giant cupcake.

MOTHER: An adorable cupcake! *(grabs a dress off the rack)* Now go try on this mermaid fit.
SAM: A what fit? *(rolls eyes and picks up the dress goes back into fitting room)* I don't see why I even have to go to prom. None of my friends are going.
MOTHER: Every girl needs to go to prom! Isn't it fun trying on all these dresses?
SAM: This is supposed to be fun? I thought it was a form a torture!
MOTHER: Don't get an attitude with me! I'm buying your dress!
SAM: Wouldn't want to spoil that, *(mumbles to herself as she looks in the mirror)* would I?

Cut to: **INT: Dinner Table**
Sam's grandfather sits at the head of the table and is talking about politics again. Her father, who is sitting at the other end of the table, is getting agitated. Her grandmother sits silently, as she and Sam have just cooked the meal and will later also be cleaning the dishes and the kitchen.

GRANDFATHER: And that's what's wrong with this country! These kids think that whatever they feel and believe in is valid! And another thing, too-- women are taking the jobs men were meant for!
SAM: *(laughing)* And what jobs are those, Grandpa?
GRANDFATHER: Women were meant to work in hospitals and nurseries! They are ruining the system! Women were meant to be obedient to men and that is the way it should be. Too many women are going out and getting jobs when they should be at home watching the kids!
(at this point Sam gets up, clears her spot and leaves the room)

Cut to: **INT: A CLASSROOM**
Sam is sitting in a desk near the back while two different colleges introduce themselves and talk about how great the social lives are on their campuses. One school is black and red and the other is blue and red, not that Sam cares.
SAM: *(aside)* Is it rude to get up and walk out? I mean, this is a total waste of my time.
RED AND BLACK: We have the best....what was it again?
BLUE AND RED: Dorm rooms? You guys have great dorm rooms.
RED AND BLACK: Yes...dorm rooms... AND SORORITIES! We have great Greek Life!
SAM: And, on that note, I'm out. *(gets up and puts the pamphlet back on the table and leaves)*

Cut to: **INT: BEDROOM**
Sam is wearing a Led Zeppelin t-shirt and ripped jeans. She is reading a book on her bed, and she is lying on her back with her feet propped up against the bedpost. It's her birthday and her mother's side of the family is coming over for dinner. Grandmother enters.

GRANDMOTHER: *(sees Sam and grimaces)* Samantha, that's not a very lady-like way to sit.
SAM: *(laughs)* Well, I am not very lady-like and I told you to call me Sam.
GRANDMOTHER: But Samantha is such a pretty name for such a pretty girl! Do you know what men like? Ladies. If you want a husband, you'll have to learn to be more lady-like.
SAM: I don't want to get married
GRANDMOTHER: That will change as you get older. Just wait. You ARE going to put some clothes on, right? (*laughing*)
SAM: I am currently wearing clothes....
GRANDMOTHER: Don't get smart, you know what I mean. Here. *(hands Sam a bag from DressBarn)* I was going to give you this as a birthday present, but you...obviously need it now.
SAM: What's wrong with what I am wearing? It's not like we're going out to eat or anything.
GRANDMOTHER: YOU have guests coming over for YOUR birthday. Show some appreciation.
SAM: Whatever. *(reluctantly takes bag)*
GRANDMOTHER: Be ready by five-thirty. *(exits)*
SAM: (*Takes dress out of the bag and puts it on. Stands in front of mirror.*) I have tried so hard to hold the same beliefs as my parents, as it is all I have ever known. But there is a point where I just can't do it anymore. What I feel... what I know... I simply can't ignore it. I don't feel right. When I am around my family I just feel like I am hiding, even though they all say, "We know you better than anyone." I know that they don't and they never will truly know me. Everything I believe and stand for contradicts what I was raised to believe. I am tired. Tired of being told which path to take, tired of being told my dreams are just that: dreams. I dream that one day I will get to work on movies every day. *(grabs the ripped jeans and puts them on under the dress)*

Cut to: **INT: Bedroom**
Sam is packing bags for college. The room is barren, there are no sheets on the bed or posters on the wall. The floor is covered in boxes and she is packing her clothes from the closet.
MOTHER: *(calling from kitchen)* Are you about ready to go? The plane leaves at five.
SAM: It's only one o'clock, but yes. Just one more bag. *(looking at the dress she her mom made her wear on her 17th birthday)* I won't be needing this anymore. *(hangs the dress back up in the now empty closet, turns the closet light out and closes the doors. Calls to her mom)* Ready! *(Before leaving the room, she grabs a map to New York and a camera bag.)*

Cut to: **INT: Film set**
Sam is setting up lighting and cameras. She is wearing a Led Zeppelin t-shirt. She sets up a tripod and points the camera on it towards a green screen with three people sitting at a dining table. A grandfather figure sits at the head of

the table, while a father figure is sitting at the other end of the table. A grandmother sits on the side by a teenage girl wearing the same Led Zeppelin shirt as Sam.
SAM: Ready in three, two - *(all three begin to clear the table).*
FADE.

*****

The Art of Life by Allie Tkach

"One ticket please." I ask the woman in the ticket booth. She hands me the ticket and I walk through the doors into the art gallery. I head to the first room, where the exhibit title reads *Life*. The room is a small one, the floor is a glossy oak wood, the walls are a plain, stark white. I look up to the ceiling; there are bright lights hanging on wires, casting light on the pictures. I finish looking at the pictures in this room; they all depicted the first three years of a girl's life.

I walk into the next room, which is covered in a mural. The floor has been painted to look like a summer lawn. Greens swirl around, creeping up the bottom of the walls. Bright, tall sunflowers with rich, yellow petals reach towards the ceiling. It was painted to look like a Carolina blue sky with a wispy cloud here and there; it reminds me how, as a child, my mom painted my ceiling to look like the sky. At night I would look up and cloud watch. I look at a picture; it's of a little girl sitting in a garden of flowers. She smiles without a care in the world. In all the pictures that I have seen so far, she is smiling. The farther I get in the room, the older she gets. There is a contentious type of picture that appears time after time, her as a veterinarian. Some of them are her imagination and others look like someone is asking her what she wants to be. At the very end of the room are what look like her middle school years. Again, the pictures of her wanting to be a veterinarian show up. I smile at how sure and dedicated to this idea she is. There are also pictures from other people in the gallery. Artwork from people like M.C. Escher and Vincent Van Gogh. I think this is an interesting mix; they fit her somehow. One full of emotion and passion; the other precise, and thought-provoking. In almost all of these pictures she is listening to, or playing, music. There are ones of her playing the clarinet and piano. She looks at peace when she is playing an instrument. I can relate to her with that; I always listen to music or play an instrument. It is a way to escape reality, much like reading a book.

The next room I walk into is titled "Stress," and from the walls I would say that's accurate. The walls are gray and black with writing in what looked to be a white marker. The words were brief: *Stay calm, Breathe, Four more years, Three Years, Two years left*. There are also song quotes strewn about. As I look around, it looks like high school. Throughout freshman and sophomore year she looks very sure of herself. The pictures are in a nice, orderly straight line, showing good grades, friends, and classes. The pictures are bright and full of life. Many show thoughts of college and careers. Well, I say careers, but there was only one career in particular. She seems very set on what she wants to do and knows exactly how she's going to get there. I walk to one of the pictures; it's of a college fair. She is there looking at colleges. I look closer, somewhat taken aback because she looks like a freshman. "This girl is very determined," I think to myself. The only colleges in the pictures are Tennessee, Clemson, and the University of Georgia Athens. It's shocking she's already narrowing down schools, but then again she has known what she wants to be since she was eight. Further down, I find pictures of what I assume is her mother. It is clear from the pictures that this girl's mother was a big part of who she is. In many of the pictures they share expressions and mannerisms. Every day they talk for at least an hour, just the two of them. However, I find pictures of her mother lecturing a boy around the age of 16 or 17 about school and college. In the picture she was not lecturing the girl, but I guess because the girl sets very high standards for herself; she took what her mother said to heart. The girl, based on her report cards, works hard and gets good grades. She begins to think of other jobs she could do, mostly ones relating to languages in some way. Until now she has seemed to be a quiet, well-behaved, stay in the background type of person. I start to notice that changing. There is a picture of a teacher on the wall; the plaque underneath reads Mrs. Murdock. In a different picture the teacher is encouraging the girl to enter a contest, Poetry Out Loud. I had seen photos of her at marching band competitions, but that was a group. This is the first time in her entire life, from the pictures I have seen, that she has done something in front of a crowd by herself.

The first picture of her as a junior is her freaking out. Her schedule is messed up and she doesn't have band. As I had seen in the previous pictures, this was a big deal; it was her class where she relaxed. She also has AP U.S. History, Pre-calculus, and Chemistry all in one semester. The only non-core class she has is her Film and Literature class. The beginning of the year's pictures are in unorganized lines and groups on the walls. A lot of them are of her stressing over math and chemistry, classes in which she is not the strongest. There are also pictures of her average day in a schedule. Wake up, finish homework, go to school, band practice (which came with its own set of problems), eat, start homework, sleep, repeat. On Wednesdays and Fridays she didn't have practice and spent those days catching up on APUSH work. I can tell from the pictures she was exhausted. In quite a few, she was crying. It's not that it was so terribly hard, but that she put so much pressure on herself to be the best. The pictures show her friends getting the best grades, being in the top ten of the class, she was not. I can tell that most of her stress problems were her own doing. She is very ambitious and is striving for perfection, which is impossible. I can see from the pictures that she puts so much stress on herself to be the best at everything she does and it ends up hurting her. In a few of the pictures I see her getting so overwhelmed she just doesn't do what needs to be done. Other pictures were scattered between the photos, but these were her own art work. They are on paper or on her arms: intricate, detailed zentangles.

Again it shows me how much attention she pays to little things and how perfect she wants them.

I walk to the next room most of it is roped off, because it isn't finished. The walls are just starting to be painted. Small sections of faded, purple, yellow, pink, and orange are blended on the wall like the beginnings of a sunrise. Further down the walls are still a starch white color, pure and untouched as if the pictures there are in a dream. I can see the pictures that are closer very well. In these she is taking the ACT, filling out college applications, and finishing high school. The pictures farther away are hard to see and make out what she is doing in her life. I can tell some of the pictures are of her in college, but I can't tell what school it is. Farther into the room it is darker and I can tell there are more pictures, but not what they depict.

I open my front door and find my husband. "How was the gallery?" he asks. "It was good. I really related to the girl in the exhibit." I reply. "Why?" my husband inquires. "Well, on first look she seemed very confident and sure of her life, but the older she got the more unsure and wary of her path she became. She was very apprehensive of her future and I was like that in high school." "Why do you think she was so worried?" he asks. "Because," I say, "she was so sure of her future for so long and then realized there is so much more to the world. In the exhibit it's easy to see how controlling she was and she most likely felt like she was losing control of her future plan with the numerous ways she could go in life. But I'm sure she will be fine in the end. Like I said, I was just like her, worried and unsure of my future, but very determined and willing to work hard no matter what it was, and I turned out happy with my life. After all, that's all that really matters in the end, right?"

*****

Lancer by Eric Wells

Two loud cracks echo through the air as I feel one massive impact to my chest followed by a second--I've just been shot. Then my body jolts as I wake up to my alarm blaring throughout my bedroom. The clock says 8:00am. With my eyes half open, the bright green numbers on the clock are making it that much harder to open my eyes and turn off my alarm. I am finally able to reach my arm over and turn it off. As my heart's still beating at a million miles an hour from my dream, I throw my body back down on the pillow and take a deep breath. It's time to start my day.

I can smell a fresh brew of coffee waiting for me in the kitchen. As I am just about to get out of the bed, I get a call from my partner saying that there was a mass shooting in the mall. I try to push him for more information, but he hangs up before I finish my questions. Since I know that whatever happened was extremely bad, I need to hurry up and get to the precinct. So with all the energy in my body, I rush to the bathroom and quickly shower off to wake myself up, then I run to my bedroom and throw on my uniform and my shoes. Since there is no time to finish my coffee at home, I decided to take it with me. I check my pockets for my phone, keys, and wallet, which are all there. Now that I know I have everything, I rush out the door running towards my squad car. Right when I hop in, I throw on my seatbelt and switch on the siren and lights. Going as fast as I can down the streets without jeopardizing anyone else's life, I make it to the precinct.

Once I make it inside, my partner Chase tells me we need to go into the debriefing room. As I walk in, my captain starts to give us the rundown on what happened. Apparently a gunman with an assault rifle of some sort, not yet identified, was dropped off at the front of the food court by an accomplice. We were not able to identify the car's origin or the shooter for the shooter was dressed in all black from head to toe, gloves and mask included. We could not identify the car other than it was an all black Chevrolet Tahoe with tinted windows past the legal limit and the license plate number was covered up by black electrical tape. This was all caught on the mall's security camera outside of the food court entrance.

The shooter runs into the front entrance of the food court as the internal cameras to the mall record his every move. As he busts into the food court, he jumps up onto an empty table and yells out, "Where is your beloved law enforcement now?" Since all of this happened so quickly, most people in the food court had no time to react. Before anyone could comprehend what was going on, the shooter started his horrific acts onto the crowd of people. During his assault on the innocent, he is shot in the arm and leg by a security officer who wasn't as lucky to make it out alive. At the end of the video it shows the shooter walking back out of the mall as the black SUV pulls up and the shooter climbs back in.

After the video, our captain dismissed us and we were dispatched to the location of the shooting. When we pulled up to the mall we noticed first responders, camera crews, and bystanders along the perimeter. As we walk in we are overwhelmed with the aftermath and Chase became speechless. Since we are still out of the loop on the casualty count, I walk up to a forensic specialist and ask him how many victims there were. He informs me that there are thirty-four, thirty of whom are deceased and four in critical condition. As I am walking around I notice a group of detectives in the food court near Stanley's Pizza so I decide to walk over there to see what was going on. There were two bullet holes one in the drink fountain and the other in the counter. One of the detectives informs me that these were the result of the security officer's shots at the shooter. One of the detective's phones rings, and I overhear the conversation between the two. Apparently the forensic team was able to identify the shooter from a blood spot outside of the mall at the location where the shooter jumped back into the SUV. The name wrings out of the small speaker at the top of the phone. "Jeremiah Lancer.". Once I hear his name I immediately pulled out my notepad and wrote it down so I wouldn't forget. I told Chase to stay at the mall and help with anything needed. Now, what I am about to do is very irresponsible, but I want this man in custody and I want to be the officer to do it.

I drive back to the precinct and run to our database. As I type his name in only one result comes up with a police record in our county. Jeremiah Lancer had been convicted three times with domestic violence charges and two times with controlled substance charges. It was also noted that he was an active member of the American Nazi Party. Then right there beside his name is his address: 789 Westcreek Lane. I write it down and head back out to my car. I put his address into our navigation system and immediately drive over to his house. Once I get there I notice there is no car in the driveway and all the lights are off in the house. I started to think not to go in because of how undisturbed the house looked, but I proceed anyway. I walk up the stairs to the front door and knock on it. I waited a minute or so and knock again, but with no surprise, there wasn't an answer. With my suspicions I reach for the door handle and twist it and notice that it isn't locked. Now I know I have to go in. I withdraw my firearm and tactical light and proceed to open the door. I quickly check my right and my left and find no threats present. As I walk down the main corridor of the house, I check every room with a glance. Something catches my eye down the hallway as I am walking. I notice the bathroom door opened with the light on and a pile of bloody rags lying in the floor. Walking closer to the bathroom I hear something moving behind me. Two loud riveting cracks echo through the air as I feel one impact to my back and the second to my....I can't think of where the second went...everything is black...what's happening to me? In the darkness I hear a sound like a siren. This noise gets louder and louder as I slowly become more conscious of myself. I open my eyes and I see my iPhone laying on my desk chair beside my bed. It is emitting the most annoying and disappointing noise I know: the alarm. As I grab it to turn it off the time says 10:30am and there is a new message on my screen. It's from my teacher letting us know we have advisory today, which means I don't have to be in class until 11:40, granting me ten more minutes of alone time. With a sigh of relief, I lay back down and think about the dream I had and how I can't wait to serve my community as a Law Enforcement Officer.

THE UNKNOWN

I'm Not A... by Nathan Ballew

Read this.
Yes, read all of this.
Every last word.
No, I'm not writing a bad haiku, because my English teacher would have a fit with my rhyme scheme.

The next step. The next step in my life is...college, degrees, marriage, kids, 401k, retirement, grandkids, old age, pills, death. It's all the same. Everyone else in this book is writing about their next step and I'll bet that most of them are all the same. Our teacher said to write about the next step. She said it could be just getting through the semester or the year or about college and careers. Everyone has big plans, or so they think. They will become doctors and lawyers, accountants and nurses, judges and artists, movie producers and software writers. I, too, will write about my future.

A scary looking fellow just walked on past by the window. I met a strange lady and she made me nervous. Everyone has anxiety. We fear when people look at us and see us during every breath we take, look behind us to make sure no one is following every move we make. Every smile we fake distances us from the greater social good which is honesty (thanks, Sting). Of course every time we distance ourselves we have anxiety from lying to our friends and family however, I do not have anxiety because if I have it it is in my possession I control it. I do not have anxiety, I am overwhelmed with anxiety. I have so much anxiety that one might wonder if I am neurotic because I am the one who peers over his shoulder, I am the one who fears the poisoning of my food, I am the one who fears the next step. What is my next step? Because I can't make it. Everyone writing in this book will make his own step and in a land full of Christians, of which I am one, some will say that God is on their minds. 'God direct me,' they say, then they go about setting their minds on worldly goals and disregarding Jesus's words on being conscious of their spiritual needs. "It does not belong to man who is walking even to direct his step," Jeremiah 10:23. Truly my goals are to pursue spiritual things. But to the reader who simply doesn't care, to the reader that does care but has no time, and to the reader who doesn't care and doesn't have time, I'll spare you the intimate details. In short: learn a new language, preach to others, strengthen the brothers. My hope doesn't lie in this world, but you don't care. I'm simply black ink on a white page. So read this, read all of this, and move to the next page about a girl who wants to be a doctor and go to college and go the the one after that which is the same story and to the next which only differs because it's a boy this time and he wants to be a mechanic, and every page is the same and I'd quote Billy Joel just to see if you're still reading and maybe "Piano Man" drifts through your head.

Everyone will write how they're non-conformists to society then write the same words as everyone else. Some are hopeful and believe that they'll do better and some will write of challenges. And I'll bet the girl next to me will quote *Firefly*. I'm not going to a big college, I'm not going to do x or y. I'm simply going to write this and show the futility of words on paper and how little they will affect change to the masses unless the masses want to believe and not just laugh at the hopeful work of some gullible teenagers. Their goals are rooted in realistic, attainable goals, but it's all the same.

However, perhaps you say, I can't only preach, for how will I get money? So I must aspire to some worldly goal, but I don't. Perhaps I'd like to be like my father who is a truck driver, which is not a glamorous job but they have CB radios, which I like. Or maybe I could be a plumber, or a mechanic, but now I sound like the commonplace writer who aspires to a worldly goal. Whatever it may be, I'll figure something out. For now I just have to focus my energy to get out of bed in the morning. And finishing this essay.

In the *Cheers* episode "Coach in Love Part One," Coach Ernie Pantusso says, "Irene, I'm not a rich man, I'm not a young man, I'm not a handsome man, I'm not a tall man, I'm not a strong man, I'm not a talented man, I'm not a well-traveled man, I'm not a smart man, I'm not a milk man, I'm not a fat man, I'm not a gingerbread man, I'm not a…"

Much like Coach, I don't have some special talent, I'm not much of anything, but I'll find something. Maybe one day I can finish the statement not as I'm not a… but I am a…

*****

Twenty by William Binkley

People step all the time. People take physical steps, steps in life, and steps in our mind. One might ask, what makes up one of these steps? Steps rule our physical world, as well as our mental world, and move our lives forward. People do not really think about what makes up steps or what steps to take next. Legs help us to step forward, but do people really know how they help us make our next step?

Humans begin standing on two legs. Pressure is applied to one's muscles and bones to help the person stand in an upright position. In order to propel one's body forward with their next step all of their weight is shifted onto one leg, the left leg. The right leg, the leg without the most pressure, is then raised. The toes also play a role in this step taking process. This is known as the toe-off phase in which the foot prepares to separate from the ground. The heel leaves the ground first followed by the toes.

The next phase is the swing phase. In this phase the leg has left the ground and has begun the walking action. This leg is stretched forward into a walking position and is dropped down. The heel is placed down with the rest of the foot following through. The right leg is now stopped in a position known as the recoil position. This position is displayed as the knee being bent and the lowest point of a walking stance. The knee bend absorbs the shock of walking into the next step. The person moves forward into their step and continues walking. The weight is then shifted onto the aforementioned right leg and the left leg is lifted. The process is repeated, but legs are not the only body part involved in making a next step.

Hips, shoulders, and the spine are also involved in taking one's next step. One must have balance in order to walk and balance is placed on the hips, the body's center of gravity. The hips rotate on an axis connected to the spine when one's leg is moved. The shoulders provide the balance on the upper part of the body. When the right leg is moved forward, to take one's next step, the left shoulder moves forward to counter hips movement and keep one's body in balance. Once the right leg has been placed on the ground, the left leg is raised and the body adjusts to uphold balance by moving one's right shoulder forward. When the body is not in motion, however, the shoulder and hips remain level to maintain the balance of one's body. The spine holds these parts together and remain relatively straight.

The head is used in taking a step, first, because humans must use their brains to walk. The head is used view where a person is going, it takes a step to make the next step. People decide where they are going by looking around their surroundings and making the decision, or taking their next step, on where to go. The head will also move around, because of the rotation of the body, to, once again, uphold the balance of the body. This is not the last thing that helps people take their next physical step.

The arms move in a pendulum motion in conjunction with the shoulders. As the shoulder rotates, the arms move with them, further maintaining balance. This helps keep the body move in sync with the steps being taken. The arms, the head, the spine, the shoulders, the hips, legs, knees, feet, heels, and toes all are involved in taking one's next step.

One could also compare this to life. When humans are born they are taught to walk and adjust to walking. As the legs become more developed, walking becomes much easier. Much like the legs, as the mind has more experiences, decision making, or step taking, becomes easier to do. As the leg muscles become more developed, they are able to withstand more pressure. Of course, all struggle while attempting to walk, while some struggle more. People go through life making decisions and while some can decide and move on, others can't decide or struggle more to decide. The mind acts in a similar way and when the mind develops fully, it can comprehend more knowledge. For example, if a child decides to touch a hot stove, the child will be burned. Since the child's mind now registers that the stove is hot, the child now knows to not touch the hot stove. Much like how the heels and knees absorb the shock of landing on the ground and follow through, the mind can relate. The death of a loved one provides a shock to the mind. The mind must process that they will be without the loved one and must continue on in life without said person. The mind must mourn and then follow through to continue taking the next steps in life.

Why am I telling you this? Well it's a grade that I needed to do on time. I didn't feel like revealing myself to you, either. I looked up all this information about anatomy to come up with 835 words about taking a next step. No, you will not know why I named my essay "Twenty." I confuse people to humor myself occasionally. You can ask me in person about the title, but I will give everyone who asks a different answer.

I have no idea what my life will be like in the future. Quite frankly, I hate thinking about it; it gives me more stress that I don't need. I hate thinking of all the possible outcomes because adults put so much pressure on knowing and commenting all of the aspects of your future. I want to focus on now and get good grades, make better choices, and learn to better my future. The adults that want to put more pressure than necessary can fight me.

I just know my future will be sarcastic and full of more people that think I like them when, in reality, I don't. I think the future will be amusing seeing people and how they view me versus how I really am, if they ever get to know me. People see me differently once they get to know me, which is usually a funny reaction. If you ever want to know something about me come talk to me. Take that next step.

*****

Onward & Upward by Cooper Brown

When choosing a career, there's no clear choice. Each individual has their own skill sets and interests. Some people are mathematically inclined, so they'd make good accountants or something else in the corporate world. Others are good with their hands or better with applied skills, so they'd be better off in an engineering field or as technicians. And then there are those who are physically or athletically inclined. They'd fit into the athlete scene such as football, soccer, track and other competitive sports. There are so many skill sets, and each job out there requires the precise combination of specific skills in order to succeed in that field.

I, for one, am musically inclined. I play guitar (yes, electric and acoustic--if you can play one, you can play the other) and I like to think I'm decent. And by the time I'm out of high school, I'll be better. Also, I can sing. I personally don't think I can sing worth a damn, but everyone else says I have a great voice so I'll go ahead and use that to my advantage. My dream job, just like every other teenage guys is at some point, is to be in a rock band. To share my art. To tour. To make an exceptional salary. And most of all see the world. I want to travel and make a good life for my family. I'd take them with me and share my luxuries with them. I'd also go visit family. Mostly in the Netherlands, from my mom's side. I just want that life so badly but I don't know how I'd go about getting there. However it does help that I listen to the music a lot. Like...too much. It probably isn't healthy. But why not? I enjoy it, and anyone who tells me not to was a kid at some point. They should understand. It is hard to get recognized in this day and age though. It's mostly who you know, or who just happens to be there when you're playing in some coffee shop in a city square. And I'm not going to get a stable career out of luck. I can't trust that some record producer is just going to hear me playing some day and say, "You're hired!" I just can't hope for that, it won't be enough. So I'd have to go to the label and talk to the producer. Or mail in a demo or something. I'm only sixteen and I'm not really sure on how to do all that, so it'll have to wait.

Perhaps I'll be a personal manager for a band. This position represents musical acts and guides all aspects of an artist's career. Their pay is conditional; I could get ten to fifty percent of the artists' earnings. However, most only get ten to twenty percent. Or maybe a tour coordinator. As a tour coordinator I oversee and coordinate all the elements and personnel. The pay would obviously depend on who my employer is, but the salary ranges from thirty five thousand dollars to one hundred and seventy five thousand dollars.

Another career field I would like to go into would be psychology. There's a lot of money to be made, and I enjoy helping people. Making people happy. Seeing people smile and knowing I made it happen. It brings me more joy than most anything, and I'd love to make a living out of it. But first I'd have to go to school for it. Preferably in-state or a surrounding state. Winthrop is a local college and has a good reputation. However the graduation rate is fifty three percent, which upon further investigation, I found wasn't that bad. Another choice is North Greenville University. I've been to the campus on youth rallies and I like what I've seen. But I have never attended the campus during the school season, so I really don't have a fair opinion of the school. They also have a thirty nine percent graduation rate, which in comparison to Winthrop, doesn't look so good. However, I also have to consider which field I want to go into within psychology.

I'd like to go into Clinical Child Psychology. I find the way that children, whether five years old or fifteen, understand situations to be very interesting--

how they rationalize or attempt to remedy problems. They don't often take all the consequences into consideration, which leads them to come to more obvious solutions that we may not have come to realize otherwise. They think differently, not necessarily better or worse than adults, but differently. But sometimes that leads to bad solutions. Fixes to problems when there was no problem to begin with. The patient may think that the worst has just happened, and there's no way to fix it, so why try to? And more often than not, the answer is to keep trying. To make it better. But no one is going to take me seriously if I don't have a degree in the field. Nobody will hire me to make a kid better if I don't have a degree.

Today, more often than not, you need an education for both fields. To be in a band I probably wouldn't, but the label may prefer me to have a degree in music theory or music production. But it's more likely that I'll need it today, like I doubt that Jimmy Page, James Hetfield, or Slash had degrees. But now, it's required for almost any job. And I'd hate to lose the life of a rock star just because I didn't learn how to do it. It doesn't seem fair to me. If I'm good at it, why not hire me and let me do it? It sounds simple enough, but that's not how capitalist America works. So I guess I may have to wait an extra four years.

As for psychology, I know I'm going to need a degree. There are fields in psychology that don't require a license, but they also don't pay as much (and I wouldn't have a long enough essay if I said I'd just apply for one of those jobs). Like I mentioned earlier, I'd probably attend Winthrop University, it seems like a good choice. However I will seek out guidance in choosing a college. Probably my parents or teachers involved in the fields that I am interested in. Hopefully they can give me substantial insight.

I don't know which path to choose. One is realistic while the other is my dream job. I'll probably end up spending a long time chasing the dream of being a musician, but I'll end up having reality slap me in the face and tell to give in to the psychology field.

*****

This Cookie Doesn't Crumble by Noah Cooke

The Next Step. Right now, it's impossible to know what it is, but two steps in the future, when you look back, it will be so obvious. I don't know what that next step is for myself, and I don't know what to tell you right now. Now I could suggest a bunch of stuff, but I think that's arbitrary and not worth anything. The next step is right in front of us. I know mine is somewhere deep down, but I don't know if I am ready to make the dive to find it. I kind of like where I'm at right now, and compared to where I was when I first wrote this mentally. I felt alone, like a lot of my friends had left me behind to go on to better (or worse) things. A lot of people have changed between my 10th and 11th grade year. Some of the changes I really like, but more often than not, I don't like change. I think I have a fear of changes; I like living in my plastic mold where I can count on everything to go as it usually does. I don't like it when people fight and they stop talking, especially when they talk about each other to me or with me around, because I don't want to choose sides. I want them to get along again, or at the very least quit talking about the other. It's crazy how I can be best friends with someone, and the next day I don't even want to think about them, much less talk about them.

Social anxiety has probably been one of the most crippling things for me. I'm flat out bad at talking to people and getting my point across, because I stutter when I get nervous and I get nervous when I want to say something. There isn't anybody that I feel comfortable talking to, not because I think they're going to tell everybody everything I tell them, there is just something imbedded into my DNA that tells me not to. It's especially strange for me to be honest with people that I am really close with, because the thing I tell them could be so weird to them that they don't want to talk to me anymore. High school has always been somewhere I was afraid to be myself, not because I would fail my classes, but because the people are ruthless. There seems to be no privacy, and anything you say can and be told to everyone. Even worse, nobody stands up for each other anymore. I've seen best friends trash talk each other and it doesn't make sense to me. A best friend isn't someone you should want to hate, it is someone you should want to love.

My family and I have never been close, outside of watching a movie, a t.v. show or occasionally eating dinner at a restaurant. I think that has been a very healthy thing for me, my parents being somewhat hands off. I got to be the person I want to be, not like Neil Perry in the movie *Dead Poets Society*. I would love to be a doctor of course, but want to be a doctor on my own terms, not because I have to be one. I like freedom as an individual, and my parents not influencing me too much has really allowed me to develop into a free-spirited person. Of course I do have some parental rules: don't do drugs, don't drink, be home by a certain time, chores, a lot of the typical stuff for kids my age. What I have come to learn is that the point of my parents giving me these restrictions is not to keep me from doing the typical youth things, but to keep me from doing the non-typical adult things. They don't want me to do it as a kid and that be the only way I know how to spend my Friday night, rather they want me to understand what it's like to still be a regular teenager.

Adulthood. It seems so far off, but I can almost touch it and pull myself to it. Almost. All that stands between me and the rest of my life is a few weeks, a semester, and another year of high school. Then maybe some York Tech classes, a job that I should feel lucky to have with my experience, and a small one bedroom one bath apartment or house. I don't really want to live at home because my brother is 23 and still lives at home, and that just isn't for me. It's kind of pathetic, how he cannot handle his own life and still needs Mom and Dad to help him do everything, whereas I am pretty independent, and I don't ask them for much besides groceries, a little financial help and a place to live. Don't get me wrong, I love my brother. He's my brother--we take care of each other. However, his life has taken longer to advance than mine will. I'm only sixteen, but I pay my own gas, sometimes my own dinner, and for my own clothes. I think that a lot of people say that kids aren't able to take care of themselves at my age, but that feels a little wrong to me. I can take care of myself for the most part, but that's excluding taxes, living costs, and all of that.

Maybe this is only the next step, but all steps lead to another. I think the most important thing out of all of this is to keep taking steps, don't get stopped because you failed a test, something went wrong in your life, or because someone is trying to hold you back. The moment you stop taking steps is the moment you get stuck. Don't spend too much time worrying about this step, because the next one is right behind it.

*****

But What Now? by Jacob Emmons

The next step. The future is always uncertain. You never know where you'll end up or what will happen next. Every step forward you take is a step into the darkness, into the unknown. Nobody quite knows exactly where it will take them. The next step is always a step into what you can't see or prepare for.

As I take the next step, I realize that maybe the future is as scary as everyone makes it seem. Maybe every step further into these uncharted waters is more dangerous than the last, and everything I've worked for might be lost in an instant. Maybe everything I love will vanish in a puff of smoke, leaving me alone and empty on this dark path without a light to guide me. I realize that I don't know where this next step will take me. What if it takes me down to failure? What if it crushes the things I love and care for? What will I do then? If failure is a possibility, why even take this next step? Why even try when you know you might not make the right move? The future scares me, being unknown. It scares me to think of the risks and what I might lose. I always overthink everything. But why overthink it? Why not just look at the future head-on and take that next step?

As I take the next step, I realize that maybe the future isn't as scary as everyone made it seem. Maybe the future isn't an endless abyss of despair. The next step I take could take me somewhere great. I could be a billionaire CEO of a corporation, or in a profession that lets me travel around the world. Whatever this next step is, maybe it will take me somewhere that I want to go. Why step in this direction? Why not take a step in a completely different direction than this? It's completely up to me, I don't have to listen to anyone else. That's how Dad did it, and that's how I just did it. This decision could be the best one I ever make, and I don't need to worry about what's going to happen. Anything that happens, happens. This decision could be the one that takes me to the top and lets me make an impact on my future. If this step is the one for me, then why wouldn't I take it? Why not give this step a chance? Why would I hide here and not let the steps I take guide me to where I am meant to be? This step could take me to college or it could take me to starting a business on my own. I don't need guidelines to tell me where to go anymore; I'm no longer a kid, unable to make decisions on my own. I'll take this step when I feel ready to take it on.

This next step is another step away from where I am, though. It's a step away from comfort, from home. This next step could take me away from my friends, and my family. I might lose people who once meant the world to me. What if I don't want to lose them? What if I want to keep these great friends that I already have? Our next steps could take us away from each other and I wouldn't see them again. These people I have forged a bond with, and this life I have that I don't ever want to forget, why would I walk away from it right now? I love where I am now. What if I don't feel like that later? What if everyone else moves on to their next step and leaves me all alone? What if I am the one leaving all of them behind? This next step is morose. It's a dividing step that can take away everything I've built and everyone I've loved. I just wish that others could take this step with me. I don't want to be alone. I want to be with these people I love, I don't want to lose these people that I've developed a bond with. I might take this step and lose them, and then what? What does the future have for me then? Why don't I just take my time before I take this step, and let everything stand still for a while, just to let myself love them for a bit longer? I hope that in our next steps that all of our paths cross again. These people have given me a reason to stand tall and take this next step, no matter where it takes me. But for now, I want to take my time and experience the people and things I love while I can.

Why does everyone expect me to go take this next step so suddenly? Why can't I take my time? They are always pressuring me to take this next step, never asking what I want or what I like. They always tell me what they think is best, and they never let me be the one to decide. It's as if everyone believes that they know more about me than I do, and that they know what's best for me and I don't. I wish they would just let me choose my own path and stop trying to decide everything for me. Who are they to decide what is best? Why do teachers and adults who have already taken their step from my position get to decide that they know what's best? Everyone takes a different step in a different direction, so shouldn't I get to pick mine? I shouldn't have a direction forced on me, I should get to choose how to step. "Oh, but what if this next step causes you to fall?" What does it matter to you? Don't you know why we fall? It's so we can learn to pick ourselves back up. I'll get back up and keep walking on in a new direction, shaping my own path and making my own maps. I shouldn't be forced into a mold that grownups set out for me. I'm not just a cog in the machine, I'm a person. I'm different from everyone else and my steps and my actions should show that. I mean, do I look like a guy with a plan? I won't take a step in the direction that you force on me unless that's the direction I want to take a step in. I won't do what you tell me just because you think it's what's best for me. I am not what you make me, I am a composition of what I do and what steps I take.

I'm not sure how to feel about this next step. I'm unsure if I'm supposed to be scared, curious, sad, or angry. I just want to know that I am able to keep going through all of the steps to come. I want to be able to look at the future and all of the uncertainty and have some sense of preparation. Maybe that comes with age, maybe as you get older and more experienced, you can become more secure in who you are and the steps you will take. My uncertainty towards the future will cause me to be a bit more cautious in my decision. I will make choices that will help me to be the best man I can be, undefined by adults who think they know best. I know that no matter what step I take I will take that step wholly, and will not let uncertainty stop me from giving it my all. All of my previous decisions have led up to this, and I am ready to take the next step.

*****

Going for Goal by Michael Gleaves

While on the field in the last game of the season, my adrenaline was pumping, everyone was yelling, and the score was 2-1. It had been a tight game, but we felt that we could pull off the win. With ten minutes left, we began to get sloppy and too relaxed. The other team has the ball heading straight for goal. They score. We are in shock; the last game of the season and we may end up losing because now the momentum is in favor of the other team. Now with two minutes left, the game is still tied. We are nervously trying to keep them from scoring again but our defense breaks down and they score again. The game is over. 3-2 loss. Playing in that game I was not thinking of the future at all. I did not think that the game we just lost could be my last. But the time is approaching for me to decide if I will play soccer again next year, my senior year.

Last season was rough. We had so many issues in our season that I'm rethinking playing soccer for our school again, a game that I love. The first of many issues came before we had our first game. Our managing director walked up to our coach in the middle of practice and told us that we could not play on our field anymore because it is too dangerous. There are too many rocks and someone would get hurt. We had practiced and played many times on that field without an issue, but this past season it was taken away. Now don't get me wrong, the field is not in good shape, but it was OUR field.

This is where the next issue starts to come along: where will we practice and play home games because we do not have a backup soccer field that we can play on? We are now forced to play in the grass lot in front of the campus, which is not regulation-size and has no lines. After the first game, our coach had even more disappointing news: We cannot have any home games this season without a home field. Half of our games are now wiped off of our schedule, just like that. Starting out with a 24 game schedule we were cut down to 11 games for the season, and they are all away games. This was heartbreaking because neither my friends, girlfriend, nor parents could come support me. The majority of our games were at least an hour away and they started too early for my parents to be able to come because of their work schedules, so I played these games without anyone supporting me in the stands a lot of the time.

The next issue came along about halfway through the season. With our athletic budget very low at my school, we don't always have a bus to games because other sports like volleyball or cross country may need it that same day as well, and this meant that we had to carpool. One day we had a game that was about 45 minutes away and no bus. I was travelling with my friends Sean and AJ, and we were enjoying the ride. Almost to the field, we were in the middle of a conversation when we all received phone calls. Some of our teammates who were already at the field called us to tell us the game was canceled. Everyone was confused why because we had almost arrived at the field. We turned the car around for a long ride back to the school. We are all disappointed. Later we found out that it had been canceled because we did not have a bus to transport us to the game, and we learned of a rule that players are not allowed to drive ourselves. We had a talk with our athletic director and he told us that every game that we did not have a bus had to be cancelled because we were breaking this state rule. This meant another couple of games cancelled that would not be rescheduled. We are now down to only a few games left.

The seniors on our team had a rough season. After having many games cancelled (not including the ones that were rained out and never rescheduled), they were then told that the soccer team did not deserve a senior night or any special recognition at school because of our performance on the field. This made the team as a whole feel like we were not appreciated at all at school. In our final few games, we were very motivated to prove everyone wrong, and we won four out of our last five. But our season was still cut short 15 games, on top of all of the added issues. Overall it was very difficult not to have a negative attitude going into games and practices after what had happened.

Right now we are in the process of fundraising for a new soccer field. We just had a Color Run fundraiser where most of the profits went into the budget for the soccer field. As for the other issues, nobody is sure how those will turn out. Looking into the future, I will have to make the decision--do I want to play soccer for our school or not. I know this will be a big decision and when my English teacher, Mrs. DiMatteo, assigned this project, I knew this would be a good topic to write on. This is a big decision for me as a person going into my senior year of high school. I want to enjoy still being a kid and playing the game that I love, but I do not want a repeat of the issues that the team as a whole dealt with the entirety of the past season.

I want to play next season because it is my senior year and I will never get another chance to do high school over again. I may miss out on some experiences and moments that I will never get back in life. I have also been playing soccer since I was four years old. It has always been a big part of my life and not playing will be difficult for me.

However, all throughout high school you are told by parents and teachers to start preparing for college. You hear all about how expensive college is and how bad student debt is. Maybe I could get a scholarship for soccer. I'm not sure about that but I do have a job, and I can start putting money away for college. This past season I could not balance school, soccer, work, and a social life, so I had to give something up. I took three months off of work so I could play soccer, and I did not have a good experience dealing with all the issues we had. Maybe a reason to not play next year would be so I could work and start putting money towards college.

I would like to go to USC and study international business. When I graduate I would like to have a Master's degree in business and then work for a big corporation. I am not sure if I will be able to play soccer in college because of the skill level required and the huge time commitment that it takes. I have always been a procrastinator, so being able to balance the schoolwork and soccer plus a social life and work will be difficult for me.

I have not made my decision yet, but I know that the people around me will help me make the best decision possible and will encourage me no matter what path I make. I want to make my senior year one that I will look back on and not be disappointed in what I did. I want to look back and not regret any of the decisions I made. The rest remains to be seen.

*****

The Movie of My Life by Chelsea Ingalls

As young kids we all had different perspectives of our futures. Each one of us had one big dream, whether it was becoming the next great NBA basketball player or becoming a famous singer or actor. We looked at ourselves in the future becoming someone so great, and successful, but now the time has come where you have to figure out what your next step is in life and I wonder, how did everything happen and go by so fast? As kids, we didn't worry much about anything except what was gonna be for dinner, or who we were gonna hang out with after school, or what our plans were gonna be for the weekend. Some of us never thought the day would actually come to be in the senior class that then graduates and starts our own lives. Now being a senior in high school, reality settles in and makes me question who I am going to become in the future. That big dream I had in my head as a child isn't real life, and it's time to take the real steps that start my future.

For some of us seniors we realize that the dream we had isn't going to happen. Those thoughts and perspectives of our future we had as a child is gone because this is the time when we are supposed to start becoming who we want to be when we were older and now all the time is gone and we have no time for practicing or studying; we have to make the big decision. When we were young and full of dreams, we had all the time in the world to start learning and practicing to become great at who we want to be. When I was a little girl all my cousins were into accessories that I wasn't into such as Barbies and American Girl dolls. Luckily, I had an older cousin Stephen I would always rely on to skateboard or play videogames with while my cousins would be playing with their dolls. Stephen was a fantastic skateboarder. He would compete and win bags full of new Vans and new wheels and accessories that made his skateboard better to ride. Watching all his friends support him and always having a crowd around him made me want to become a professional athlete. I was playing soccer and spent most of my time trying to improve. I had realized I was better than what I thought I was, and became striker after my second game. I used to look up to Stephen, and he would make me believe that I was capable of becoming great at this sport. I moved on from soccer to basketball and volleyball, and I will always have sports as an important part of my life.

We sometimes change our minds on who we want to become, but starting early as kids such as playing basketball we practice to get better, so by the time it's senior year we are prepared and ready to start our next step in life. We always wish we could go back to start learning and practicing earlier so that we would be even greater when we become older, but as kids, not all of us thought in that way. I wished that I had practiced soccer more when I had first started because I had picked up basketball that made me gradually lose my passion for soccer. I had then spent more time on the court then on the field. My dad was a great athlete and had played soccer as one of his sports he pursued. My dad and I had built an even closer relationship from him taking time to teach me certain soccer skills to make me a better player. Knowing that we can't go back and change how we lived, we have to work on what we can do now and become the best we can be without wishing we had done more. When your focus is on the past you get off track about your thoughts on the future. You are then too focused on the regrets, that you miss out on thoughts and ideas you could have had about ways to become better at what we decide to put our whole heart into.

Not everyone knows what they want to become in life and I am one of them. I had my mind set on being a nurse but then changed it to being an athletic trainer. Some people say that without college you won't get anywhere in life.

I believe that college doesn't have to be for everyone. Hopsin said, "Did the man who invented college go to college? Ok then." Some people get job offers at a young age from either the family business or from a job they worked at while in high school. Everyone has a path to pursue and I believe it's possible to become just as intelligent and successful as people who do attend college. High school is the foundation, and what we do with what we learn and how we use our time is up to us. We have to make each day count by not missing out on opportunities that people invite us to be a part of.

Our view on life slowly changes as we gradually get older. Situations that come up can change our view on someone we built a close relationship with because we see the real side of them and never would have expected that they would make a decision to hurt each other. I have gone through this experience in my life with some extended family that I grew up. Like all kids, I made some bad choices and these family members viewed me differently. They were the ones that I thought I knew would always be there for me through the bad and the good. I'm actually glad they found out about my mistakes and I saw their reactions, because then I would be living my life thinking they would they would be there for me when now I know otherwise.

As we figure out who we want to be in life, we can't base decisions off of a single person's advice. We have to ask other people's opinions and then look back over everyone's advice they gave to us and then decide for ourselves what we want to do. The most important person I know that will always give me the right advice is my dad. I know this because he doesn't want me making the same mistakes he made. He listens to me and gives me examples of things that happened in his life and how he had either made the right choice or the wrong choice and tells me how he overcame it. I have also seen how much my dad has grown into a stronger person because my dad has so much respect for not just his family, but for others, too. Some people then take advantage of it and no one appreciates the things he does to bless people. Lastly, I value my dad's advice so much because I see the way he lives his life. He isn't someone who tells me to not make bad decisions and then he goes and makes the same one he told me not to. As a father he knows he is being looked up to so the decisions that he makes he thinks of me and my brothers so that we can see examples of how to live life doing good deeds and handling a situation correctly. Neither do we want to make a decision that will make someone we look up to proud of us, or to impress when really it's not something we really have a heart for because the decision wasn't based on what would make us happy. What we decide now can affects our whole future. Whatever some of us choose to do, we could be doing every day which means we need to make it worth something that we know we are going to enjoy. Having to dread doing something every single day is going to get old and it's going to affect how we act and not enjoy life.

Each person has a purpose in life. We all have a talent, but some of us haven't figured out what that talent is. We have to put ourselves out there and do things we never thought we could do or even would do. We are not always going to be young; we get old and our bodies become weak as we get into adulthood and become parents and grandparents, which means we need to live life to the fullest now. I know that my essay topic was supposed to be about my next step, but the reason I didn't write about mine is because I am still trying to figure out my next big step in life myself.

We look at the movies and see that at the end somehow the problem always gets solved and everyone is happy, but that's not always real life. We are faced with certain situations that may not end with smiles, but we do know that there are days ahead of us to look forward to as long as we make the efforts to make them the days we won't forget. Our life is our own movie and we are the producers. But the thing that is different is that our movie doesn't end until we end.

I don't exactly know if I am going to have a comical, sad, or chaotic movie for my life or if my movie will have all of these elements. But I know that I will always make the best of what situations that come my way. The good and the bad obstacles that we will be faced with as we step out into the world on our own two feet will make us stronger at who we become. Life is a gift and we need to not take it for granted. I know that everything will happen for a reason, with a purpose behind it, and that will make me grow into the person that I want to become.

*****

Life is a Journey by Emily Jackson

I'm not good at planning. I never have been. So when people tell me I need to start planning for the future, I get a little freaked out. It makes my toes crinkle up and my stomach get all knotty. I can't even choose what clothes to wear tomorrow! Since 8th grade, my dad has been telling me to get a list together on what I want to do after school, and I have. In 8th grade, I wanted to be a veterinarian. In 9th grade, a marine biologist. 10th grade, a playwright. 11th grade, I wanted to be a film director. This year, my last and final year, I think I want to be a veterinarian, again. I'm still not sure, though, and it's driving me crazy. It seems like a good idea, but what if I end up hating it? What if it's not for me? Then I spend all the money and time in college for a career I hate. I'm scared to commit to anything, but my time is running out.

For now, I think it'd be best to start with what I don't want to happen with my life. I don't want to live at home, with my parents, until I'm thirty. I don't want to skip college altogether. I don't want to join the military. I don't want to be stuck at a fast-food restaurant for the rest of my life. I don't want to be homeless. I don't want to live in the busy city, but not a lonely countryside, either. I don't want a rich, lavish lifestyle where everything I ask for, I get. Most of all, I don't want to feel like my work is work.

Now for some things I *would* like. I would like to get some level of college education. I would like to get a job I love. I would like to get married to someone I love and who loves me back. I would like to get a cat. I would love to make life-long friends. I would like to live in a cute little house in a perfect little setting. I want a life where family is not only defined by blood, but by who will stand by me when I need them most. I want a life that's not handed to me. I want a life that's my idea, not anyone else's. I want my life to be mine. Most of all, I want the life I've built for myself to be something I love. Something I can look back on and say, "There's nothing I regret doing with the time I've had." I want to enjoy it.

The idea of college scares me. It's going to be the first time on my own. I'll have to pay extra for staying in the dorms, or I'll have to pay for an apartment. I may have to have a roommate, but who knows whether or not they would keep up on their part of the rent? There could be a falling out between us, and then what? Then there's the matter of me actually doing my work. Now, it's easy to say "Of course I'll do the work! I'm paying for it!" but who knows how long that's going to last? I won't have my parents looking over me and guiding me through it. As much as I hated them hovering over my shoulders to make sure I get this and that done, I think I'm going to miss it when I leave. Being a vet would be an amazing job, in my opinion. I love animals more than anything and being able to help them if they're not at their best would be wonderful. The only parts I would not be able to stand would be euthanasia or animals dealing with abuse or neglect. Just typing this part makes me so frustrated. Animals can be the most loving and loyal things on this Earth, yet people treat them so badly "just because." I don't understand how someone can do that.

If I do change my mind again between now and college, I'd have to say my backup plan would be a teacher. Preferably high school level, but I don't think I would mind elementary level. I would love to teach History or English, my favorite subjects.

I think the thing I'm most scared about would, by far, be my independence. It sounds good in my mind: "Oh yeah! No more parents telling me what to do. I'm able to breathe easy knowing every text I send or every action I do isn't monitored! I'm free!" But the more I think about it, the more scared I get. I'm going to be responsible for judging if something is a good idea or not. I'm going to be responsible for paying bills. I'm going to be responsible for remembering important events. I'm going to have to be a responsible adult. And I'm terrified of it.

It's alarming to think that it's been almost eighteen years since I've been born. It's been twelve years since I started school. It's been four years since I started high school. This time has gone by too fast and I'm worried about how fast time will go in the future. Where will I be in another eighteen, or twelve, or even four years? How will I have changed? How will my friends have changed? Will I look back on those years regretting everything, or will I be happy? I'm trying to think of how I can plan my time to make the most of it, but it's really difficult. I'm starting to think of my life like a treasure map. I just need to follow these little plans in order to achieve this wonderful, treasured life. As Ralph Waldo Emerson said, "Life is a journey, not a destination." I hope my journey will be a good one.

*****

The Happy Step by Eron Johnson

I have always been the kind of person to try to make everyone else happy, regardless of how I felt. If everyone else is happy, then there is no worry and everything is good, right? Eventually, I was torn between making everyone happy and knowing why I had to do whatever I was asked to do. I was always inquiring my parents as to why I had to do this, or why I couldn't do that. I would ask, "Why can't I climb the tree with my friends?" or "Why can't I use the stove yet?" Whether I was told the consequences of my actions or not, I simply had to try it just once. Most of the time this would end in burned hands or bleeding legs, but I always wanted to know why things would happen. When I grew older and the word "why" became frowned upon in my life, I began to just listen to what I was told without ever knowing the reason for why. My questions were dismissed and ignored. The default answer of "Just trust me, Eron," was given more and more. People grew tired of my questions. Everyone else seemed to know more about me than myself. How can anyone know what is best for me better than I can? No matter what decision I made, there was always someone who disagreed or had a better plan in mind for me and my future.

Now as a sixteen year old senior in high school, I have finally realized that the first person I need to make sure is happy is myself. For as long as I can remember, it was drilled into my brain to make "good grades" so I could get into college with scholarships. "Every single point matters," my parents would tell me. In some ways the hard work they put into me paid off, because the summer before my eighth grade year I got a call from my school's principal. I had just transferred over to this school and needed to take a class that was not available in the lower grades. He asked me if I wanted to stay in the eighth grade and just take the class online or if I wanted to bump up a grade and take the class as a freshman in high school. I told him that I wanted to stay in the eighth grade. When I told my parents that I was offered the opportunity to skip a grade, they were ecstatic. They called the principal right away and set up my schedule. I was now a freshman in high school. We had a small celebration in honor of my success. I loved school and it was never too much of a challenge for me but now I was in high school. I asked my parents why this was so important and I was always given the same answer: "Scholarships." I wasn't sure why this was so important. I understood the idea that scholarships were free money, but didn't understand why I should be punished for not planning my future as adults seem fit. Adults and peers would always say they knew better because they had been in my situation before. Everyone is questioning me about my "next step." The infamous "What do you want to be when you grow up?" question. As we get older it simply transitions to, "What are you going to do once you graduate high school?" I have always answered this question with "Well, I'll just go off to college and get my degree." But as I got older and my interests began to change, my plans began to dissolve. After being so sure of my plans, it all began to change. I thought, what if I don't get accepted into my college of choice, or any college at all? What if I am not good enough? The idea of going away to school became less and less appealing as I would only be a 17 year old freshman in college. I wouldn't even be able to purchase a pack of cigarettes (not that I would want to). I wondered if maybe I should take a year off of school and find out who I am. I was always told that this was a terrible idea. But no one ever explained WHY.

I have three months left until I graduate from my high school. My plans at the moment are to go to Coastal Carolina University and get my bachelor's degree in Recreation and Sports Management. Instead of declaring a major for the money, I chose one that I could see myself working thirty years from now. But who knows. I have now considered four different majors in fewer than two years. The thought of choosing my career while I'm still a teenager seems completely and utterly absurd to me. I can't even choose a movie without growing bored in the first thirty minutes and switching it out for a new choice. I still have a curfew and cannot get into an R rated movie. I still want to play Xbox and go hang out with my friends at the movies. Am I truly ready for the next step? When thinking about getting to be on my own and getting to discover myself, there is not a doubt in my mind that I can handle this. When I think deeper about the responsibilities, I am not so sure. When associating with my peers and friends at school, most are set on majors and career choices, but there are a few others like me who are walking through this blindfolded, grasping and reaching for anything that seems like it might be able to help lead us to the path best suited for our future. But then I think, "Why is it so wrong to make a mistake?" The only real way we can actually learn anything is by messing up. And I am not talking about the whole "been there, done that" mess that people like to tell you; I mean real, cold, hard, painful mistakes. A teacher of mine once said to me, "Life is 10% what happens to us and 90% how we react to it." No one is going to be there to baby me once I am out on my own. I know it is going to be difficult and I am choosing the "hard way", but these are things I am going to learn.

Although I am only sixteen years old, I have learned something I feel will stay with me throughout my lifetime. No matter how terrible or miserable the situation seems, dwelling on the negatives have never solved anything. I have learned to participate, not anticipate. Worrying about the future or the past only lessens the experience of today. I am choosing to take each day one step at a time. We are all taking steps. Everyone is at a different place, going in different directions. Nobody can take this next step for me. This is something I can only do when I feel ready. As much as people can try to guide me in the direction they see fit, in the end only I can choose which step to take on this crazy path from childhood to adulthood. I think I'm ready... Well, I hope I'm ready.

*****

The Path by Kameron Midkiff

Imagine a pitch black field. You don't how long the clearing is or how wide it is or even how far the darkness reaches. Sometimes the valley becomes lighter and you can see several paths that diverge into the woods surrounding the clearing, intertwining at various points before they spider web out like broken glass. Some paths are smoother than others, little incline and almost no potholes. Some are jagged and covered in sharp rocks or have boulders blocking the end of the path.

Taking the next step, treading under the archway with 'FUTURE' curved along the top like a greeting. As stepping through the gateway, The path behind crumbles and shifts away like a river carrying the ice sheets from the winter, and I stumble from the aftershocks. There is no going back, no changing the past.

A sparse border of trees forms a straight line at the edges of the clearing becoming denser as the forest continues, creating a wall. Openings are randomly spread throughout the wall leading into to paths that venture until they become too dark to see down or turn sharply. As the paths disappear into the dense forest obstructing their final destinations, There are signs at the openings of the trails. Each gives a vague description of what each path entails—deciding where to go to college, scholarships, majors, internships, careers, roommates, an apartment—each path connects and merges or splits in different directions.

Some paths are more worn down than others, with smooth terrain and no obstructions, they are clearly much easier to navigate. Other paths are littered with rocks and debris, some have massive branches crisscrossing to form a barricade twenty paces into the pathway. Another path has colossal jagged rocks protruding from the ground like pillars, making the journey to its destination hazardous. The paths with hindrances will require more time than those that are unblemished.

The clearing slowly becomes brighter, as if the sun decided to make a minuscule appearance behind the grey clouds polluting the sky, and more paths become visible. Too many paths. They litter the tree line. Some so close together they seem to be the same until they curve away, separating. It is impossible to examine them all for the dangers they may hold.

Making a decision to choose the path less traveled by, and I start down the trail with daunting obstacles and oppositions. Wandering down the path littered with logs and branches, I reach the barrier I assess how I will overcome such a challenge. As I look at the problem, it seems almost impossible to solve or get around it. Just as I am about to give up and walk back to the starting point, I see the problem from a new angle and I find an opening and squeeze through to the other side.

Once on the opposite side, I notice the path is clear and tranquil as far as I can see. The main path shot of straight ahead of me with small footpaths branching out and weaving back into the main path, intertwining like vines. Few walkways continue out into the forest, under the towering trees until they disappear from view. A small creek trickles beside the main path, the muffled churning of water dominates the space with interjections coming from the birds hiding in the high branches, and the trees that ruffle their leaves in the wind.

Continuing down the path, following the inclines like gentle waves in the ocean, and I make my way towards the future.

> Two roads diverged in a wood, and I—
> I took the one less traveled by,
> And that has made all the difference.
> —Robert Frost, "The Road Not Taken"

*****

21st Century Scop by Troy Ray

The future is a very confusing thing for a lot of people. I am not an exception; I have a lot of trouble when it comes to thinking about the future. For instance, I have never really known what I wanted to be. When I was a kid I had big dreams like to be a politician or an astronaut, but now I have nothing but doubt because as I come to the age of adulthood, I am gaining knowledge about the world as it is. I'm getting my first real look into how it works, and it's frightening for me. I'm going from never having to do anything but school and homework to having to get a job, going to college, and getting a degree so I can get a better job. Then find someone you love to be with, then raise a family, and guide them through the same process...it's daunting. All we want is not to be forgotten when we die. Like the scops from the Anglo-Saxon times, we want our stories to live on. So I take life in small steps, in the present moment, so that I don't overthink anything too much because if I do, I will take an idea and think it to death and it usually turns out bad.

In regards to the future I am a big thinker--even though it's not helpful in some situations, it helps me delve into some deep questions about the future and life. In life, I believe there are the strong and there are the weak. This is a very common idea when dealing with people and life but they usually only talk about physical strength. I'm talking about three different strengths and compare them to myself. To begin, the first strength is mental capacity and willpower. I put these in the same category because they go hand in hand in dealing with who you are as a person. Strong willpower will let you act on the ideas you come up with so you can accomplish something great. On the other hand if you have weak willpower, then you will be trampled by someone who is stronger and you'll never get anything done. Mental capacity isn't about how smart you are--if you look at it like that, you will always find someone smarter than you. It's about your common sense, how much information you can retain, and how smart you are. It's one of the most important strengths, in my opinion. If you have mental strength you can do more and achieve more while dealing with problems and situations. I'd like to think of myself as having a pretty good intelligence, even above average for my age, and I often find myself having to explain my ideas to people with closed minds who never let anything in and push away new ideas. All I can think is, why do people latch onto an idea and kick everyone down that has something to say about it?

The second kind of strength is emotional, which is the most important kind to me. A lot of people will tell others to "follow your heart" and it will lead you to all the good things in life. Maybe, but if you focus on emotion as the only guide in your life it will end badly. If, for instance, you act a lot on emotion and something bad happens in your life, then all that emotion will stop you in your tracks and break you down. It's what emotion does: it builds you up in good times and throws you around and kicks you out in the bad times. The key is to release emotion's grip on yourself and take everything in as a problem that needs solving. I do this because emotions will cause blind faith and bad decision making, so I try to stay as if only the good emotions are there. When bad emotions spring up, I keep a cool head and take things one step at a time.

The third and final strength is obviously physical strength. Physical strength will always be necessary whether it be dealing with people or having a job. It can also give people the confidence to do things in life that others just won't do. I myself am relatively strong and plan on staying active during my life.

These three strengths do not just have something to do with life in the present, but also a lot with the future. If all of these are met, then you can be a successful person. It can let you improve as a person, a friend, a leader, but it can also take you wherever you want to go by enabling what you already have within yourself and releasing it in the world. I personally believe that I have these traits and have the ability to change the world, but to take this to heart I also have to believe that I can fail; nothing is ever set in stone. To be a good person and problem solver, you must have humility. Even if you're the best problem solver or genius in the world you won't always be able to succeed, and if you can't take failure in a good way you have to find it within yourself to move away from your faults and keep moving forward. The future is something I believe that has limitless potential. I believe as a people that we can, with these strengths, accomplish something great in this life and not just leave behind another meaningless life. I say this to show the longing in human nature to rise above yourself and become something more, to strive to be better than anyone. All we want when we die is to not be forgotten.

*****

Plastic Sparkly Sandals by Annie Robinson

I got new shoes yesterday. Plastic sparkly sandals that make me skip around and twirl and stuff. Forever 21, $10. For the purpose of this essay I'd just like to point out that since I'm currently wearing these glitzy, gaudy, glamorous things, I'll most likely be taking my next step in them. Unless by some horrible twist of fate, when I try to get up, I find that my legs don't work. Then I won't be taking any steps at all. But that's the worst case scenario.

The future is that really fast kid on the playground during recess that you're playing tag with, and every time you almost tag her, she just does a number right over your head and speeds right up and out of your reach. She teases you just enough to always keep you engaged, always keep you chasing even though the both of you know it's all a futile effort--because you can never actually reach the future. It forever remains unattainable and unreachable. But that's a good thing because that also means that it's never going to be set in stone; it's never going to be a fixed outcome. You never know which direction that kid is going to run, but you keep chasing anyways because you love the game.

Sitting in the guidance counselor's office, trying to map out the rest of your life, it's the silence. The ringing in your ears. The unspoken words. The words you can't take back. The words you can't unsay. The words you can't control. It's too much of a gamble to ever say them so you tuck them away, lay them down to forever sleep, bury them in your backyard under all the mounds and mounds of college applications, guidance counselor pamphlets, and scholarship essays. The four corners of the earth press down upon you with the never-ending pressures of everything: the pressure of yourself, and your peers, and your parents, and your financial standing; they just press down on you. Everything presses at, pushing you into the trap of adulthood, ensnaring you upon all the "real world" worries until finally one day, you aren't a girl with dreams anymore, instead you're a girl with realities. Realities like "you don't have the grades to do that" or "you can't make any money being that" or "you have so much potential why would you settle for being just that" or "there's no way you could ever make a career out of that". So you can't even speak because you're Atlas too busy holding all the pressures of the universe on your shoulders. You are force fed all the expectations and statistics, and percentages, all the numbers and facts and study cases, all the evidence that just goes to prove that Career Clusters are higher law and what you get at end of your personality test is obviously who you are. So you stay silent. You don't ever say the words. You don't ever voice your dreams. Instead you simply nod along as your counselor lays out your life according to your most compatible cluster.

I've watched high school like a movie. I've spent the last four years collecting memories and moments that have felt silver screen-worthy. Memories that fit the music: watching fireworks on the beach, screaming from a mountain top, driving fast on a freshly paved road, playing tag on a playground after midnight, taking in the view of a room decorated to look like a winter wonderland, crying on the bathroom floor, breaking plates, taking my AP exams, sinking a free throw, holding a newborn baby, sitting on my grandma's roof, standing on an old vandalized bridge, laying in the grass on a warm spring day, carving pumpkins and singing carols, watching movies and reading books, dancing and dancing and dancing. All these collective moments have fed into my high school experience, all of them building and learning from each other. For better or for worse they've all happened and for better or for worse they've all helped to create an 18 year old girl. But it's the spring of my senior year, and all of these memories are building up to the end of all things as I've known them. They've created this crescendo that has ever built up to that one last great and glorious moment when I awkwardly walk across the stage, shake hands, and walk away from high school forever, accompanied by a piece of paper. All the memories have worked towards this moment, this moment when everyone will applaud and see a finished product. When everyone will of course know that Annie has pretty much completed her transformation from adolescence to adulthood. When Annie will gleefully set off on the path towards success, having already mapped out the next thirty years of her life as a high school senior. The moments, having done their job well, will have manufactured a quality product that has sufficiently been scanned, packaged and labeled, ready to receive a safe college degree. A nice neat check will go in a box next to her name.

Or no.

Screw Career Clusters.

Really, truly, and honestly, I hate career clusters. They've come to be a realistic representation of everything I hate about taking steps in life. Would you like to know why? Would you like to know why I hate seeing the results that tell me I'd make a good teacher or a great nurse? Would you like to know why I will hold off choosing a major until the very last second possible? Would you like to know why I shrug my shoulders when everyone asks me what I'm going to be when I grow up?

It's the simple fact that I won't be defined. I won't be categorized. I will not be weighed and priced for my value to society. I won't believe the big misconception that none of us are allowed to take risks and sometimes even fail. I won't be told I can only be one single thing in this whole wide world of limitless possibilities.

My memories haven't created a model perfect professional person. They've made a mess--a beautiful mess of chaos, uncertainty and talent. They've created someone who is energetic and crazy and messy and creative and awful at keeping time. Someone who is this strange mix of slightly everything. They've created me and in doing so they've made me cringe and cry and hiss at all of these labels.

There are words that I've never said out loud. Words that I've never had enough confidence to even whisper, much less share with anyone. They are words that are a part of me. Words that I've never been able to face in the mirror. The words that I've always felt; that I've always fought with. Words that will almost guarantee failure, that will almost guarantee rolling eyes and whispers. Words that may or may not make me foolish, words that may or may not make me great. Words that I've choked on for so long, wedged in my throat, waiting to be spilled out onto paper. Words that I can't take back. Words that I don't want to take back.

I want to write.

I want to write a lot. I want to write it all. I want to share the sum of my memories, the sum of my existence. There is a comfort in writing that I can't find anywhere else. It thrills me, it completes me. I go out and I have all these transcendent teenage experiences and the way that I make sense of it all, the way that I tie all the beauty of life together, is through words. There are so many feeling and sensations and moments in life that somehow tie into each other and the way to comprehend and really understand it all, is to write about it.

You can draw your own conclusions if you'd like, because I don't have any. I feel both so young and so old at eighteen and I'm not going to conclude anything because this isn't a movie or a book, it's just the outlook of a girl wearing plastic sparkly sandals.

*****

I Breathe, I Think, I Dream by Ella Rosenberg

Every day the same routine.

I wake up, brush my teeth, get dressed, sit in my car, turn on music, exit car, go to school, enter car, turn on music, go home.

From there I do homework with perhaps a light snack in hand while I work and write for a few hours, sometimes I clean if I finish early. It's a simple autopilot response that keeps me busy. After the day is said and done, I get ready for bed and go to sleep.

The cycle continues. It seems like the only thing that changes is the weather, the amount of light is left in the day, the music I listen to. I'm a robot, a machine. I follow the patterns and dare not stray.

One day, however, it *does* change.

I forget my phone, which I always use to listen to music in my car on the way to and from school. Instead, I turn on the radio.

Global warming, wars, lost children and school shootings fill the gap between my ears. An article about the lack of education and its effect on the surrounding area ends with something along the lines of, *"This generation is our future. We need to make sure that they know that."* These words echo inside my head as I go about the day, not the lyrics of my current favorite band.

While walking along the halls of school I notice the banners and posters seem more vivid, "WHERE ARE YOU GOING?", "SIGN UP FOR THE ACT!", "DON'T FORGET THE SAT!" ... These posters make me struggle to remember my ABC's.

The conversations in passing snag my thoughts by the ear, "So I was thinking about Clemson...", "Did you hear that Rebecca got accepted....?", "I'm almost done with filling out..." The clouds in my head both dissipate and thicken as I go through the rest of the school day.

I drive home from school with the radio off, the noise in my head enough to keep me well preoccupied. More questions than answers seem to circulate in a slow rhythmic pattern, a halo of thoughts, the sound like white noise in my head.

I'm greeted by my mother at the door. She hands me a pile of envelopes and advertisements for various colleges and universities, and asks me if I've been reading them. I tell her truthfully that I had scanned a few, but not thoroughly. She shakes her head, sighing, "Well, at least read these today. You've got to start thinking about what you're going to do. The year is almost over, you know."

I nod my head and go to my room, placing my mail next to the others on my desk. I pull out my homework but I don't start, not yet. I'm too busy trying to un-muddle my thoughts to focus on the present while simultaneously trying to forget it. After debating for almost 10 minutes, I pull out my laptop and decide to browse social media to loosen up.

My friends on Facebook post pictures of their university lives, jobs, and adventures. This one is in Mexico, studying abroad and on her way to a degree in international communications. This one is taking a break from studying for her masters in biochemistry by watching the sunset on a local beach. This one is showing off her newest art thesis project, a short film about a pastel-colored mermaid wanting to attend a school on land.

I shut my laptop off and go back to homework only to have my little sister knock on my door to inform me that dinner is ready.

Everyone is sitting at the table, my grandparents are here, too. We're having my favorite food for dinner tonight, Argentine barbecue. The smell of spices and meat from the grill lift my worries away. I tune in on the dinner conversation as I help myself to some *pan y chorizo*.

My family is blended, my stepdad's side is from Buenos Aires, Argentina. When they speak, half of it is in Spanish, half of it is in English. I can't speak Spanish very well myself, but I can understand most of it. As I'm digging in, Tata, our nickname for my stepfather's father, asks my stepfather how everything is going.

"So, how is the project outside coming along?" he asks in rapid Spanish, before taking a bite of his steak.

"It's great, but I'm not really sure what to start on next," my stepdad replies (also in Spanish). "I've got so much left to do, I don't even know where to start…"

"Well," Tata begins, pausing for a moment. "Whatever it is, you need to decide soon. It's almost winter, by then it will be too late. Just start on something and then work from there. If you are overwhelmed, you can always ask for help."

The conversation drifts, some of it I can't fully understand. I'm not really listening anymore, anyway. I realize what I need to do now.

After dinner is over and I help to clean up, I bid everyone goodnight and head back to my room. I take a long shower, get in some comfortable clothes, and grab my laptop.

The hardest part is turning it on. I don't know why, it's such a silly thing, yet it is the most difficult. Once I press the button however, everything else follows easily.

I browse colleges online in place of clothing stores, I fill out applications instead of personality quizzes, and I start outlining essays instead of stories that I can never seem to finish.

The noise in my head stops. I suddenly realize I've been actually miserable since summer ended, but now I feel ok. It's like a weight that's been piling on my shoulders has finally been lifted, and I can breathe more easily.

I turn my laptop off and one-by-one the lights of my bedroom. As I settle down and doze off for the first good night's rest in I-don't-know-how-long, I start to visualize and wander into the realm of sleep.

A multitude of paths open up before me, some stretching thousands of miles ahead into the distance, some located closer to home. So many choices, all I have to do is choose one. I refuse to be stagnant. I finally know my next step forward.

I breathe, I think, and I dream.

*****

Santa, the Tooth Fairy, and My Future by Rosie Torres

When I was four, people would ask "what do you want to be when you grow up?" Well, that's easy. An astronaut, a princess, a doctor, a chef, a ballerina...the possibilities were endless; no matter what you said, the grown up would say, "Oh how cute," and go along with whatever you said. "What do you want to do when you're older?" The question gets harder as you grow up because it gets more serious. You can't say you want to be an astronaut or a princess or a ballerina because those are not realistic. "What are you going to do when you graduate?" The magical question every single high schooler is tired of hearing. Since society has decided that it is completely normal to ask teenagers what they want to do for the rest of their lives, I guess I am going to have to wing this entire thing because I have absolutely no idea what I want to do and I will admit I am 500% lost. The only thing I have been told by adults so far is just take it one day at a time and it will just "come to you." Sure. Whatever you say.

The goal for the rest of my high school years is just to graduate and leave. Why am I in such a hurry to leave? Because the high school experience is nothing like the movies and anyone who tells you, "They're the best years of your life," is a liar and I recommend you do not go to them for further advice. Of course I plan on going to college afterwards, although I have no idea what I will even major in. My plan when I was little, when Santa and the tooth fairy were real people, was just to get married and live in a ginormous pink mansion with endless halls and shiny chandeliers with my Prince Charming husband. I stopped letting that be my plan when I found that I could become insanely rich on my own and boys are dumb. My plan now is just to graduate with decent grades (because, let's be realistic, anything better than that is beyond my capability) and to go to college at Converse and figure everything out then. I know for sure I'm going to take the Politics of Harry Potter (yes, it is a real thing and yes, I am very serious about it).

The question they should be asking high schoolers shouldn't be, "What do you want to be when you grow up?" but, "Who do you want to be?" By changing out that one word, you bring out real ambitions, not default answers driven by how much money they're going to make. It's the truth, honest and simple. The possibilities will become endless again but this time they'll be real and they'll seem tangible. You can say, "I want to be the ballerina who lives in New York and does shows on big stages." If I say, "I want to be the happy girl with cats and hot chocolate who dances in her pajamas," people will laugh at me and say, "No seriously. What do you want to do?" The more specific question is not only going to give you an honest answer but the other person will really appreciate it, too. It makes us feel like you actually care about our interests and you are not just making small talk because you really don't have a clue on what else to do. Believe it or not, teenagers really do care about the future, so much that sometimes we panic and self-destruct in an implosion of procrastination on studying or filling out college applications. We are terrified of the future because everyone puts so much stress on it. Yes, it is important. Trust me--you don't have to tell us twice. Sometimes we need a breather, though. Deciding the future is not any easier with a financially-secure adult breathing down our necks.

Who do I want to be? I want to be like Malala Yousafzai and advocate the importance of female education in countries where it's questioned. I want to be like Princess Diana and go past the boundaries of everybody else's comfort zone to bring light to real problems in the world. I want to be like Margaret Thatcher and do things that people think only men can do. I want to be a human and animal rights activist, a world changer, and a feminist. I want to be a feminist like Beyonce and Chimamanda Ngozi Adichie. Last but not least, although I want to be like these women, I also want to be myself. I don't want to end up being one of those people with ambitions at a young age who forget all their goals when they're older and end up having a job where you are chained to a desk with a sad plant and a creaky office chair. I want to make a difference somewhere, anywhere, for anyone.

My third step is to remain optimistic throughout everything. I have learned that pessimism only holds back what optimism could potentially bring forward. It's a simple lesson, one that took way longer to learn than it should have but I'm confident I'll use it for the rest of my life. The only three steps I have right now will be stepping stones for my future and hopefully will help me with all my other steps.

Perhaps you don't need everything planned out, maybe all you need is three steps to get you through everything. People have done much crazier things than graduating and having no idea what to do. I already know that no matter how much you plan and make steps, life is always going to say, "Not today, Bud." It's only going to get more difficult from here, but these steps have helped me with everything so far. All I need for right now is ambition, optimism, and of course, a sense of humor.

*****

What to Do? by Bailey Youngs

As high school students, the one question we despise more than any other is, "What are your plans for the future?" A lot of us have no clue what we want to do for the rest of our lives. It's such a tough question to be answering when we have only caught a glimpse of the real world and have experienced maybe a part-time job and very few responsibilities, like paying for gas, or your own clothes, or your own car insurance. Of course, the normal response is "go to college" or "get a job" but that is just scratching the surface of the adult life. There is so much more to it than what we can really grasp. I know a lot of seniors brag about how they got accepted into a big fancy college but have no clue what they want to major in. They might say "I'll figure it out while I'm there," but I think that's a lot of money to be spending to maybe figure out a career choice. Personally, I think that when you go to college, you should go with a career field set in your mind. A lot of us are forced to go to college, and what for? There is no point in paying all of that money and doing unnecessary classes just to say, "Oh, I went to college," when your future isn't guaranteed. It's a big risk that ultimately puts a lot of people in debt, if they even make it to graduation. I've known several people who dropped out only one or two years into college, take nothing away from it, and end up working at Bi-Lo or Publix. What amazes me is that little piece of paper that costs thousands and thousands of dollars will get the job, even though he might not be the right person for it. You could know every single little thing about a job but what good is it if you can't take the knowledge from the books and apply it to the job? College might make you smart, but it doesn't make you a good worker.

I'm sure everybody has heard the phrase, "If you do what you love, then you never work a day in your life." This is true for my father, who is a contractor and has done this his entire life. He told me that he loves to take old and worn-out kitchens and bathrooms and bring them back to life. He installs new floors, and cabinets, and with the help of the rest of his team, painters who paint the walls to the electricians who install new lights that light up the new room. This has sparked a little bit of interest in me as I have been to work with my dad numerous times and I like the hands-on, and the craftsmanship that the job requires. Every time I go to work with my father the people he works with tell me what a hard worker he is and how similar he and I work. But my father told me to never do what he does, He would much rather me go to college than work all day breaking my back while I sweat to death in the sun. Despite how much he doesn't want me to follow in his footsteps, he now owns his own business doing what he loves.

My mother is a server and I'm not really sure that she loves what she does, but she makes money and puts food on the table for us. Some days she comes home complaining about co-workers or some of the people that she waited on, while other days she comes home in a good mood. She has been doing it almost all of her life, so I guess she can't really dislike it too much. In my very near future I want a job where I wake up and the first thing I think about is how much I want to go to work today, I want to make a difference no matter how big or how small, I want my future to be useful not just for me but the people around me. Of course I want to make money--everybody wants to make money, I just haven't quite figured out what is something I love to do and something that will pay the bills at the end of the month. Right now, I am working with my mom as a server and our co-workers also tell me about how much they like working with her and what a hard worker she is. But I strongly dislike it and don't see myself doing it after another month or so. My plan right now is to go to York Tech and try out different career fields and see if anything sparks my interest, such as welding, automotive technology, or a couple of other career fields that I've never experienced before. Maybe one of those will spark my fire; if not, I'll keep on trying different career paths until I find something that I could see myself doing for the rest of my life and be well off.

As graduation is approaching and I'm no longer going to be in high school, and I'm about to go into the "real world," it's actually kind of scary. I think about all the poverty, all of the stress about paying bills and working, and trying to get by each and every month. Honestly, I'm ready for the challenges that are going to be thrown at me. I'm ready to be an adult and make choices for me and only me, but with that freedom comes responsibility, and that I don't think I'm quite as ready for. So in order to have a good life and be a successful adult, I need a good job that pays well and in the field that I love. I'm thinking once I find a career field that I am interested in, I'm then going to go to college, taking classes that will help me be successful in the future with my career. Then once I graduate college and go hunt for a job and stick with it for a little bit because chances are, like most jobs, it is going to suck, but if I stay with it and stay focused on what I want to achieve, then I'll be set for life: living the American dream with my beautiful wife and two kids with a big house, green grass and a big pool in the backyard. All I have to do is take the next step.

Postscript

The End Is Just the Beginning

Our time here is coming to an end,
Just one more step before a new life begins.
Just eight more classes before a degree
Then we're thrust into life's reality.
We say goodbye, we part ways.
A new path has opened for us to embrace.
That path is long with some turns ahead.
It goes up a hill and then down,
Twists one way then another.
It takes us back yet forward again.
There will be forks, corkscrews, and tunnels,
But the light always shines ahead.

We move on in life,
Always walking forward,
Yet never leaving the past behind.
The past cannot be changed,
But the present and the future can.
There will always be mistakes,
It's how they're used that counts.
Don't dwell on them
Learn from them.
Use them to become a better you.

Our lives are about to change forever,
No moms to tell us to take our medicine,
Clean our rooms, do our homework.
No fathers to save us from the things that go bump in the night,
Laugh with us over the silly things,
Teach us all they know
And help us when we need it.
They will be there for us always,
But now we have to learn to be there for ourselves.
The end of high school is near,
A new life is waiting for us.
It's dark and cold and terrifying,
But this end, is just the beginning
And a new path is lighting up.
We just have to be brave enough to take it.

--Victoria Gaston, class of 2018